Unanimous Praise for *The Go-Getter Girl's Guide*

"Every woman can appreciate a few easy tricks to look and feel her best. . . . Packed with spot-on style and career advice to help you look great and be successful."

—Sara Blakely, founder of SPANX

"A must-read book for savvy women everywhere. Debra's invaluable style and career secrets are sure to skyrocket you to success!"

—Shoshanna Lonstein Gruss, president of the Shoshanna clothing lines

"Go-Getter Girls know that 50 percent of their credibility comes from how they *look,* 40 percent comes from how they *sound,* and 10 percent from what they *say.* Debra Shigley provides practical tools and tips for achieving 100 percent success at Go-Getter Girl speed!"

—Lois P. Frankel, Ph.D., author of *Nice Girls Don't Get the Corner Office*

"So much more than a series of success stories . . . This kind of wisdom is priceless. With her keen understanding of today's working girl, Debra explains how to put those street smarts into practice."

—Carley Roney, cofounder and editor in chief of The Knot Inc.

"Take the workplace by storm! A fun step-by-step primer for getting everything you want out of your career. Shigley shares tips from leading women professionals for navigating your way through the 'real' world, including networking, projecting the right image, dealing with office politics, and negotiating for the plum jobs you deserve. If you have ambition, this book will give you the confidence and tools to go out and make your dreams happen."

—Bonnie Fuller, former editor in chief of *Us Weekly*

"A fast and fun read for the busy on-the-go girl who is looking for her 'must do' tips for success!"

—Keri Glassman, nutrition contributor to CBS's *The Early Show, Women's Health* columnist, and president of Keri Glassman, A Nutritious Life, a nutrition counseling and consulting practice

The

GO-GETTER
GIRL'S *Guide*

The
GO-GETTER
GIRL'S *Guide*

GET WHAT YOU WANT IN WORK AND LIFE

(and Look Great While You're at It)

DEBRA SHIGLEY

THOMAS DUNNE BOOKS

St. Martin's Griffin

New York

While this is a work of nonfiction, some individuals' names and identifying characteristics have been changed. These names are noted by an asterisk.

THOMAS DUNNE BOOKS.
An imprint of St. Martin's Press.

THE GO-GETTER GIRL'S GUIDE. Copyright © 2009 by Debra Shigley. Foreword copyright © by Nancy Lublin. All rights reserved. Printed in the United States of America. For information, address St. Martin's Press, 175 Fifth Avenue, New York, N.Y. 10010.

www.thomasdunnebooks.com
www.stmartins.com

BOOK DESIGN BY AMANDA DEWEY

Library of Congress Cataloging-in-Publication Data

Shigley, Debra.
    The go-getter girl's guide : get what you want in work and life (and look great while you're at it) / Debra Shigley. —1st ed.
        p. cm.
    ISBN 978-0-312-55575-7
    1. Women—Vocational guidance. 2. Career development. 3. Job satis...
4. Success. I. Title.
    HF5382.6.S487 2009
650.1082—dc22   2009012121

First Edition: September 2009

10 9 8 7 6 5 4 3 2 1

Dedicated to my mom and dad

Contents

When I was in preschool, a boy named Seth Kosto announced that purple was a "boy" color. He said it with confidence. No, he shouted it out loud. Suddenly, an entire color—including its shades of magenta, lavender, plum, and aubergine—was off-limits to the girls. I was gutted. Purple was my favorite color (and my grandma's too). Within seconds, I was underneath the table. I crawled to the other side of the room, unnoticed by the gang of boys now grunting and cheering beside Seth. I reached up and snatched a handful of Crayola crayons. Then I ran, fistfuls of purple in each hand held high over my head: I had liberated the crayons.

Yeah, the story is funny. (Although I think my parents were actually called to the school to help calm me down.) But it's also quite telling: I was born a Go-Getter Girl. It's just who I am.

To be perfectly honest, it hasn't been something I've always liked about myself. It can be hard to be "outspoken and ambitious"—or "focused and strategic" as some people prefer to describe us. Sometimes, I think that it would have been easier to sit back and not really go after what I wanted in life—to be a get-along girl, as Debra says. Sure enough, there were plenty of girls who sat there happily scribbling away with pinks and oranges while I ran around the room like a pint-sized Crayola warrior.

However, I'm wired to leap. When I was miserable in law school, I knew I needed to do something to change my situation. I didn't whine about it and mope (okay, well, maybe I did for a minute!). But then, the Go-Getter Girl in me took charge: I threw myself into something positive and tangible, starting Dress for Success, an organization that provides work-appropriate clothing for low-income women. I started the organization in my apartment, armed only with the ideas that good clothes were important in the work world and that everyone should have access to them and a $5,000 inheritance from my great-grandfather. My first move wasn't to write a plan or conduct market research. Instead, I talked to people. I shared the idea. I took lots of meetings. I listened. And, most important, I acted. Within a year—and still not a penny more raised—we launched Dress for Success. And within two more years, we were in more than thirty cities nationwide. One thing I learned from this? Every time you want to say the word "but," switch it for "and." There are so many reasons to be a get-along girl, and you can choose to be a Go-Getter Girl instead—and this book will show you how.

This is an important book. Now I've got a name for what I am: a Go-Getter Girl. And, better yet, I'm reading about loads of women who are wired the same way. Sounds like a movement!

The best part about this book is something Debra didn't say explicitly: Go-Getter Girls embrace the fun in life. Seriously. I mean, she's got a chapter here called "Natural Beauty is Bullsh★t!!" Running throughout this entire book is Debra's sense of humor—along with the notion that being a strong, successful woman means taking things in stride. It's the chapter she left out and instead included throughout each one: laugh. Her sense of humor makes this book engaging, and laughter makes life much more enjoyable.

My two cents? Read this book. Buy it for a friend. Discover and celebrate the Go-Getter Girl in you and in your girlfriends, coworkers, sisters, and neighbors . . . and do it with a smile, and perhaps with a cocktail in your hand.

—*Nancy Lublin, CEO of Do Something and founder of Dress for Success*

What It's All About

Chances are if you picked up this book, you've always been something of a go-getter. You're someone who's cared about doing well in school and in your career, and you've worked hard—and excelled—throughout high school, college, maybe even grad school. You may have even graduated at the top of your class, with an accolade-packed résumé, and have lined up a sweet job at a Fortune 500 company. Finally, that golden door to "your future" edged its way open, and you entered the work world.

But then, all of a sudden, you found yourself asking an unfamiliar question: Now what? You probably never expected that you'd be feeling a little . . . lost. And it was only the beginning.

For many of us young women, the path to "success" starts out so very clear. In school there are grades, trophies, rankings, and degrees. There are timelines and deadlines for what we should be accomplishing when—not to mention a set schedule of where we need to be, what classes we need to take, and what concepts we need to master, at least as a starting point. A friend of mine who is now a successful reporter at a major newspaper puts it like this: "In school, it was always so clear what was the 'right' thing to do. You do the reading and the homework professors tell you to do. If you get a B+, you go see the teacher, make the corrections, and, boom, perfect paper. If you're good at it, you can go through all of your schooling with few mistakes and get nothing but praise. But then you get out there in the real world, and it's just not like that. It's a lot less clear when you're on the right track."

As you may have already discovered, navigating the work world can be a constant question mark—and the things we as young women obsess about range from the major to the mundane and back again. On any given day, you may have wondered things like: How can I get that interview at my dream company? How do I impress my boss? Are these pants too tight for the office? Do I join in to my cubicle mate's gossiping or tune it out? Can I leave early for my yoga class? Is this job right for me, and what job should I be looking for next? Is it okay to go stockingless in the summertime? How can I make sure I get assigned to that coveted account or project? Should I ask for a raise?

If you've ever asked these questions—or it hasn't occurred to you to ask—then this is the book for you. This guide is not a gentle primer on the world of work. It is not a manual for "getting by" at the office or being an average employee—not that there's anything wrong with those goals. What this book is, is a practical guide for what it takes to *get ahead* in your career—and to create the job and life of your dreams—and it is founded on a set of simple, time-tested principles that work. This book contains those essential secrets, those of Go-Getter Girls: the driven, stylish, successful young women (many of them famous) who've "been there, done that"—recently. Through commonsense wisdom, *The Go-Getter Girl's Guide* will help you on your road to professional and personal success, and in it you will find a no-excuses, big-picture way of thinking about your life and career, as well as specific, day-to-day strategies for how to:

- navigate the tricky terrain of office politics
- find and use a mentor
- figure out when it's time to get a new job (or career)—and have the courage to act
- dress (and groom!) for success
- take care of yourself physically and emotionally
- and much more

Sometimes, no one is there to tell you how to format a business letter, much less put one foot in front of the other to achieve all of your long-term career goals. But let's face it, if being successful were so easy, everyone would be! Every young woman would have the exciting, fulfilling, challenging job; great salary; and thriving social calendar—not just a select and seemingly lucky few. And, deep down, you want what *those women* have got! Being in the "middle of the pack" is simply not enough. You want to excel—maybe even be a star. You've already learned that getting what you want out of life is about not just working harder but working smarter. All of which is why you picked up this book.

Maybe you've thought, If only I could chart out the directions when it comes to my career: how do I get from point A to point B, and what is my next step? As you know, in the working world, the answer can be far from obvious, but one thing is for sure: achieving your dreams does not happen by accident. Along the way, we all need a bit of guidance and, sometimes, a ton of inspiration. I hope this book will provide you both, along with a possible answer to help you solve virtually any work-world conundrum you may face—a Go-Getter Girl's answer, that is.

Curious? Well, let's get started!

Part One

GET STARTED

AS A

GO-GETTER GIRL!

1.

The Birth of the
Go-Getter Girl

The summer before my senior year at college, I really wanted to be lazy. No more shamefully underpaid journalism internships for me. I had spent previous semesters toiling practically wage free at places like *Dateline NBC* and *Fast Company* magazine. But this summer, I thought, I'm just going to *have fun*. In retrospect, I think this was code for, I'm about to graduate from college and I really have no clue what I want to do with my life or how to go about it, so I think I'll just procrastinate a little longer! I took up a friend's offer to move to New York and share a sweet rent-controlled sublet in Midtown, and the day after I arrived, I found myself a hostessing job at a hip downtown restaurant. There, the staff was a perfect slice of New York's glittering, glamorous, wannabe life. The bartenders—all tall, dark, and Appaloosa-like—were "models"; the predominantly blond, buff, and all-American waitstaff were actors and singers; and the hostesses, a mix of exotic-looking beauties, were all dancers.

The weeks passed, and I scurried along, delivering menus and crossing names off the always-pages-long waiting list, less fazed than the rest of the staff by the occasional celebrity sighting. (When Keanu Reeves showed up, you'd think the president had arrived!) Less fazed, that is, until one day a lesser-known-boldface name walked in: Soledad O'Brien, then the host of NBC's *Weekend Today*.

"Oh my gosh, do you *know who that is*?" I gushed to my fellow hosts, all hyperactive and borderline girl-crush. But I didn't approach her. My gut told me not to disturb the famous lady with a stroller, hubby, and what appeared to be in-laws in tow. The next day, however, I was sitting in a park outside my apartment, feeling a bit bored with the hostessing gig, and at the same time a little ballsy, and I thought, Oh, what the hell, I'm going to write her a letter. I got out a pen and *hand*wrote a three- or four-page letter, starting with the oh-so-original phrase, "I've never written a fan letter before." I told her how much I admired her work, then explained my interest in television broadcasting and my experiences as a summer intern at two news outlets. Finally, I said that I didn't have a clue what to pursue after graduation and asked if she would ever be willing to chat with me. I included my phone number and address and sent it off to Soledad O'Brien, c/o *Weekend Today* at Rockefeller Plaza—to what I figured was surely a black hole of weirdo fan mail and never-to-be-opened press kits.

A few days later, I was sitting in my apartment, watching MTV, when the phone rang. I picked up—okay, you know what's about to happen—and heard a chirpy, television-toned voice at the other end. "Hello, is Debra there? This is Soledad O'Brien." I couldn't believe it! She said she had received my letter and asked me to come down to the show and have lunch. I was speechless. Days later I found myself sitting in the *Today Show* studio at 30 Rockefeller Center, and then at a restaurant with Soledad. (She ate a monster hamburger, confiding that she had just found out she was pregnant with her second child.)

Soledad was all business. Her first words when we sat down were a brisk, "So what do you have for me?"—meaning, fire away with the list of questions I was sure glad I'd prepared: How do I break into the field? (Producing, not on air.) How important are looks? (Very, but everyone will want you to change something so you just have to get over it.) How can you manage work and family? (You make it work.) At the end of our little meeting she generously offered to let me come visit whenever I wanted throughout the summer. I accepted her offer and went to visit every few weeks. Soledad set up mini-training sessions/informational interviews with other members of the staff and crew, and she let me sit in on some meetings and hang out with her behind the scenes, including when she was getting her makeup and hair done. She even started referring to me as her "faux intern." Who could have known that a simple, honest, handwritten letter would lead to such an invaluable introduction into the world of TV news?

I certainly didn't at the time, even if my instincts helped me stumble in the right direction. It wasn't until after I entered the working world, first as an entry-level video journalist at CNN, and then as an editor for *Atlanta* magazine, that I made a startling observation: some women *do* know a set of unwritten, nearly second-nature rules about how to go after what they want and get it.

MEET SUZANNE

Suzanne is a young woman who, say, just started working at your office. She is smart, savvy, sophisticated, and stylish. She walks briskly into the conference room with a sparkle in her stride. She opens her mouth to speak, and all eyes turn, backs straighten, and everyone pays attention. Her words, filled with substance and thoughtfulness, pour forth polished and with just enough precision. She has presence—vibrance even. Above all else, Suzanne appears to be self-aware. But at the same time, her charisma is completely sincere.

As she speaks, you're wondering (hoping?) whether there is anything wrong with Suzanne. You glance from her ensemble (a tidy navy Nanette Lepore–looking suit) to her hands (which, if not manicured with some pale pinky color, are always neatly groomed) to her shoes (fashionable spectator heels with just a splash of pizzazz). Even the folders of documents she's using for her presentation that day are placed in front of her all neat and organized—not unlike her entire office, you've noticed, which remains relatively clutter free even during deadline week.

The degree of Suzanne's substance and style is so impressive that, at first, you are—oh gosh, it kills to admit it—a little *intimidated* by her. Naturally, part of you wants not to like her—she's just *too* poised and polished! She can't possibly be down-to-earth, you think. But then you see her in passing around the office enough times to challenge that initial impression. She's always smiling, and you'll occasionally spot her in the break room making conversation with everyone from your boss to her secretary to the interns about, say, last night's *American Idol* episode. And then you're assigned to work on the same team as her for a project. She's filled with ideas on how to get the job done (when did she find time to do all that extra research?), acts respectfully and appreciatively to everyone on the team, stays later than you and comes in earlier when it's crunch time, and even volunteers to organize the food and beverage runs. Of course, she simply wows the bosses with the final product. You see that Suzanne is ambitious and focused, but you start to realize that she's just plain cool. In other words, she is *so not* a b★tch.

Then, seemingly out of the blue, you hear that Suzanne got the coveted promotion to a new division of the company, complete with a 30 percent raise and a fab new Managing Director title—and she's only twenty-eight! You really want to hate her, but you can't. You respect and admire her too much! And, it's so clear to you that Suzanne is not Miss Perfect. She's just a go-getter—that is, a Go-Getter Girl.

After I'd been in the working world a few years, I'd met quite a few Suzannes—but at the time I hadn't quite realized the shared character-istics among these distinctive women. Instead, you might say that the Go-Getter Girl was born a few years later on a beach in Cabo San Lucas, Mexico, where I was vacationing with my former college roommate, Jenn. It was one of our regular cross-country—or in this case transcountry—get-togethers in which Jenn, and a handful of college and postcollege friends, and I would update one another on our love lives, swap style advice, share war stories about work, and generally plot the course of our various hopes and dreams.

In our years as recent college graduates we'd already observed the differ-ence between certain types of young women in the workplace. There were the women, like Suzanne described above, who just seemed to know certain stuff about appropriate workplace behavior, how to socialize and network and how to always look great while they were at it. Then there were other young women who seemed frazzled, self-conscious, or easily dispirited—who stumbled to find their footing in a professional environment. We wondered what the Suzannes had in common—which factors set them apart from their less proactive colleagues. Jenn and I started to brainstorm women who typi-fied this all-around ambitious mentality, along with a certain fashion sense, poise, and grace. I thought about gals like Sara Blakely, the still-under-the-radar founder of Spanx, whom I'd met through work, and my mentor Soledad O'Brien. Jenn threw out some names of people who were successful but perhaps known for having a queen-of-mean personality or perhaps were not so stylish.

"Yes, maybe," I said. "But you see, I'm thinking about young women who seem to have it *all* going on—they're stylish, successful, sassy, maybe even sexy. Definitely super smart—what's the 'it' about these women?" I mused, sitting there on the sand, as Jenn splashed in the waves. Then Jenn looked up and said, with the crystal clarity of those Pacific waters, "They're Go-Getter Girls!" And that's when I knew I had to write a book based on this unique breed of young women.

Later, after I returned from Cabo, I sat down and decided to research the etymology of the term *go-getter*. I immediately went to the place where all research vague and specific begins nowadays: Google, of course. After a few clicks, I discovered that the word *go-getter*—a phrase I had heard people use often around places like CNN and Harvard (where I'd attended college), and that I had assumed was a hallmark of modern-day, go-go-90s ambition or dot-com-whiz-kid success—first appeared in American English around 1910. Online dictionaries defined the phrase as "an ambitious enterprising person" or "a person disposed to initiate action, rather than take instructions" or (a definition I particularly liked) "a person with a strong drive to accomplish useful goals; especially, one whose career progresses rapidly." Just like the Suzannes, I thought. There is even a 1921 story written by Peter B. Kyne called (what else?) *The Go-Getter: A Story That Tells You How to Be One.* I immediately went to Amazon.com and ordered it.

Kyne's story is about a young man trying to make it in the sales business. The man's name is Bill Peck, and he is a wounded veteran who lost part of his arm and broke his leg in battle, forcing him to walk with a slight limp. Peck goes to see the curmudgeony old founder of a logging company, in search of a job, and the story follows how, despite his youth, his handicaps, and his lack of credentials, Peck proves himself to win a coveted position as a manager. I finished this brief novella—it's just about sixty pages, plus an additional dozen pages of updated material by business writer Alan Axelrod—and thought, it's a fine tale about persistence and general business acumen, but did it speak to the unique challenges that young women who are go-getters face in the workplace? For guys, succeeding in the working world may not be simpler, but it's certainly different. Guys don't worry about what happens if you start to cry at work—it's just not gonna happen! They don't fret too much if they have an issue with a friend (or frienemy) at work; they talk it out, have a beer, and all is well. Men don't feel as much anxiety or discomfort when they ask for a raise or promotion; no one ever told them it's "unmanly" to ask for what you want—whereas we may have heard that it's "unladylike" to do the same.

Whether it's politically correct to say, a young woman in the workplace today must deal with an array of issues that men simply don't face. She has to figure out how to navigate office politics while dealing with the *Mean Girls*-esque gossip scene that plagues many workplaces and how to shape her image as a strong, focused leader without crossing the line into b*tch category. She has to find mentors, whether male or female, in professions that may still be old-boys' clubs—carefully avoiding the perception she's a tart when those mentors happen to be male. On top of all that, she must tackle daily wardrobe issues, like the all-important question of how to eliminate the tummy bulge in her killer wrap dress. And whether she's in a boardroom, a courtroom, or a newsroom, her smarts and statements will likely be judged as harshly as those outfit selections. Let's face it: we live in a world where a tiny blush of cleavage by Hillary on the Senate floor is the subject of *Wall Street Journal* articles and a top story on cable news!

Modern young women want it all when it comes to work—they want to be success stories instead of squatters; fashion mavens instead of frumps; and, maybe, on occasion, the most popular girl in the room. Did the *Go-Getter* tale address all that? Of course not. There is something to this notion of the go-getter spirit that is timeless and true, but in reading the book it was clear that the rules for men (um, circa 1920) don't really apply to today's young women.

However, like the fictional Bill Peck of the 1920s, there are many real, modern women out there today who are able to triumph over this seemingly endless array of minor and major obstacles, finding the jobs and building the lives of their dreams. My position as an associate at a high-powered law firm later on in my career only confirmed this insight. Even though I didn't quite know what I was doing that summer before my senior year in college, I later saw from observing my female colleagues that not every woman would have felt emboldened enough to write that letter to Soledad O'Brien—or, as Ms. O'Brien had more dramatically done years earlier, leave school, take a job at a local TV station, and work her way up and around the country to land a national-network job by her early thirties. Indeed, many young women tend to "go with the flow" instead of taking the initiative to go after their goals. Many miss out on plum projects and aren't sure how to turn things around and impress their bosses. Many get stuck in the mud of office gossip and lose sight of the big picture of their careers. These get-along girls, as I came to think of them, often have the best of intentions, but they simply don't know how to navigate the often-treacherous working world.

MEET JULIE

Let's talk in more detail about the get-along girl, and for the sake of argument let's call her Julie. Julie is a smart, nice girl with great potential—but right now, she seems like a good candidate for a makeover on one of those reality shows. Julie is a little anxious and self-conscious, even frazzled at times. She's stuck in a job she really doesn't enjoy, but she can't quite determine how to get out of it, or she keeps getting passed over for a promotion but usually finds herself paralyzed by fear when it comes to navigating the next steps of her career. Julie might be seen at work pouting more often than smiling, distracted more often than engaged. She lacks initiative, some would say, but perhaps doesn't really even know what "showing initiative" means!

When it comes to her clothes, Julie is not quite put together. For example, maybe her pants are constantly dragging on the floor, her sweater is faded and pilled, or her black pants and too-revealing tank look more appropriate for a nightclub than a boardroom. These fashion faux pas probably result from lack of know-how, not from lack of care (though this may be the inadvertent message she is sending, as we'll explore below).

Other young women? They know that success does not happen by accident. *They're* the girls who get the swanky job—and the promotion and the raise—when everyone else is lamenting the bad market. They're the ones who have a social calendar brimming with exciting friends and jet-set adventures when everyone else can barely fit in a workout or a haircut. To top it all off, their outfits always look so damn put together, and you'd swear they spent a fortune and three days getting ready. These smart, savvy, sophisticated young

GGG Quiz:
What's Your Type?

Are you a GGG or a get-along girl? Read the following statements and ask yourself if they are true or false.

1. I never gossip at the office.
2. I have great mentors that I consult regularly.
3. I almost never break down in front of others at work.
4. I'm strategic about my career—tactical, even.
5. I'm not afraid to take risks when it comes to my career.
6. I regularly get compliments on my clothes at work.
7. I have several beauty rituals for what I consider "maintenance."
8. I know how to "informational interview" and have done it often.
9. I've asked at least once for a big raise.
10. I usually wear some makeup to work.
11. I own a control undergarment.
12. I eat healthy and exercise regularly despite my crazy schedule.
13. I take the initiative to talk to people I don't know at parties.
14. I'm currently in my dream job (or pretty darn close).

If you answered "true" to most of the above, you're on the right track to being a GGG. If you answered "false" to more than a few, then you may inadvertently be stuck in get-along-girl land. Either way, keep reading for how to break through and fulfill all of your GGG potential!

women are what I have come to call Go-Getter Girls, and my goal in this book is to help all young women unleash their own version of her.

So how can young women achieve the seemingly disjointed set of characteristics that epitomize the idea of Go-Getter Girls? Well, as I began to interview so many bona fide Go-Getter Girls, I realized, it isn't magic—it's strategy. The premise of this book is that Go-Getter Girls are not necessarily born—they can be made. Sure, some Go-Getter Girls have an inherent knack for professionalism. But for many GGGs, the secrets of the unwritten Go-Getter Girl gospel have been learned along the way, often disseminated through casual coffee talk (What should I write in my business school essay?) or emergency late-night phone calls (Please! Is it okay to wear black nylons to this interview?) with other women who are alpha girls in the work world. That's why I knew that I needed to profile the stories of real, live Go-Getter Girls—young women who were experiencing rapid success but who weren't necessarily so uberfamous or intimidating that their achievements felt unattainable. The dozens of successful women I interviewed come from many different ethnic, geographic, educational, and professional backgrounds, but as you will see, there is a common thread in their attitude about and approach to success. They, too, once felt a little lost and confused in the world of work, but they figured it out fast—and so can you! Whether you are just starting out, perhaps trying to land your first real internship, or are further along and stuck in a midcareer rut, I hope that this book—filled with stories and priceless pearls of wisdom gathered from so many bona fide Go-Getter Girls—will help steer you on your path to success.

Trust me, every Julie—every get-along girl—has a take-charge attitude that's lurking beneath the surface! In the following chapters, you'll hear from real-life women who made it happen for themselves, like Nancy Lublin, the founder of Dress for Success, who, at age twenty-three, took an unexpected

$5,000 inheritance check, an idea that came to her in an elevator, and the advice of three nuns to transform her "miserable" law-student existence by starting what would become a worldwide women's organization; Cat Cora, the Food Network chef who famously maneuvered her way to the front of a book signing with her idol Julia Child to procure forty-five minutes of life-changing advice and impromptu mentoring on becoming a chef; and Carolyn Hax, who out of sheer "desperation" wrote her way out of a *Washington Post* copyediting rut and onto a path to an advice-columnist dream job—as well as many rising stars in various competitive industries. These are women who are, to put it bluntly, making sh*t happen, and this book contains their lessons learned— along with the skills, secrets, and strategies that helped them along the way. Keep reading and you too will be inspired and able to tap into and embrace your inner Go-Getter Girl—and pursue the path of your dreams.

2.

The Work World Can Be a Cold, Hard Place— You Must Learn to Deal with It

*S*oledad O'Brien, the anchor of CNN's *Special Investigations Unit* and the former anchor of CNN's *American Morning* and NBC's *Week-end Today*, has such unflinching belief in herself that her husband, Brad, jokes that her parents must have done a *really* good job instilling her sense of self-esteem. "He always says I'm so confident—even when I shouldn't be, I really am *quite* confident!" One time when Soledad maybe shouldn't have been so confident? When she was a fledgling reporter—her first on-air job, which she'd scored after many years behind the scenes as a producer in local and network news. "I didn't really know what I was doing, and in a way, I didn't really deserve the job, but I was a fast learner," she says. "I remember walking in on a conversation once, and everyone was discussing how I got the job because I was black. I said, 'You don't think it's because I was a *network* producer?' So I had different credentials, which were valuable. But there was no question: I hadn't been on air."

Soledad remembers that at the station most of her coworkers simply weren't nice to her. Maybe it was because she was an "outsider" and they were jealous and suspicious of her seemingly out-of-the-blue promotion to a gig in a large market (although, little did they know, she was being paid a fraction of what all the other reporters were being paid). Maybe it was that she was a northerner, not a lifelong west coaster. Who knows? All she knew is that most people didn't like her—and they didn't help her. But Soledad certainly couldn't let that deter her; instead, it motivated her. It was a simple but great lesson to learn early on in her career: the work world can be a cold, hard place. You have to learn to deal with it to succeed!

Soledad's husband helped her assess the situation objectively. "He'd say, 'There are people who are worse than you in this shop, and people who are far better than you. You're not the bottom, but you're not the top. You have room to grow.'" When producers would scream at her for fumbling a report or criticize everything from her outfits to her read (i.e., the way she read a news script), she responded by coming in on her days off and weekends to sit in the control room, by herself, to screen her reels and review and critique her tape. She would analyze and devise strategies for her live shots (as her husband said, "You're trying to do too much—you need to do just three sentences in, three sentences out."). At the core Soledad was aware that, yes, she did have room to improve; that, no, she wasn't one of her bosses' "favorites"; and that, yes, some colleagues' comments were coming from a plain-old mean-spirited place. But that didn't mean there wasn't some *truth* in their comments, and she could use this experience—and needed this opportunity—to work on her skills.

Even when the hostility persisted, Soledad didn't whine to her boss about being treated unfairly or complain to HR (it may be a controversial statement, but, really, in certain workplaces, what good will that do?). Instead, she reached out to former bosses and friends at NBC. One helped give her some perspective by reminding her that these reporting jobs are hard to come by. "Don't quit," he said, "let them fire you." As for getting through each day, another friend gave her some priceless advice on how to deal: "She said, 'You need to walk in there every day like you won the lottery.' She wasn't talking about thinking of the job itself being a lottery prize. She meant, you need to learn how to *fake* being happy. 'Nobody likes to see some sourpuss walking down the halls,' she said, and, 'What I want you to do is smack a smile on your face and fake it every day.'"

Her friend explained that one method to do that is to visualize that you won the lottery—sort of like acting class where you're given a scenario. (Try it! You'll notice your face kind of lights up into a beaming smile!) "From that point on, I acted like I just won the lottery—and I could glom on to that feeling to get through it." Soledad says that while this was one of her most difficult jobs, she learned a valuable lesson: not everyone has to like you in order for you to succeed. Instead of getting guidance from her present colleagues, she sent her tapes back to her old contacts at NBC, with whom she'd kept in touch. "When they were looking for an anchor for a new show on MSNBC, I became that anchor."

GGG Nugget of Wisdom: *Not every person is going to like you in every place you work. That's okay! Accept this, assume an attitude of "fake it till you make it," and use the experience to keep building your skills and moving your career forward.*

Soledad, as her career progressed, was able to tune out the noise of workplace gossip and limit her emotional reaction to criticism, which enabled her to develop another key skill to which she credits her success: the ability to seek and accept feedback. "I always thought, if your boss is thinking something, it's great that he calls you in to discuss it, because you know why? He's having these conversations in a room without you, behind closed doors." To Soledad, it was infinitely better for her to be aware of the feedback, instead of finding out secondhand from, say, her agent. "You really want to feel that your boss can talk to you directly, so then you can *fix* the problem!"

At the same time, it's easy to get defensive and react with hostility when someone is telling you that you're doing something *wrong*. That's a human reaction! Soledad learned to "dig into" the criticism by asking questions and "drilling it down" for useful, objective nuggets of wisdom. For example, if her boss would say that her segment was bad, she would ask, "Well, what about it was bad? What didn't you like? I thought the goal of the segment was to do X—is that not the case?" or, "We have to change my thought process obviously—here's why I did this, what should I be thinking about differently?" Soledad found that if she approached receiving feedback this way, her reaction didn't sound defensive—and she wound up with a deeper understanding of the criticism instead of with someone's initial gut reaction. Plus, colleagues respected that she was really trying to figure out where she went wrong. "At the end of the day, for me, these are the people who sign my paychecks. If they think my read is bad, there's a 90 percent chance my read is bad," she says.

One time, later in her career, she encountered a truly mean person, who ambushed her with extremely hurtful so-called feedback—and even then Soledad used the experience to grow professionally. ("I'm nauseatingly optimistic," she jokes. "Everything I go into—if it doesn't go as planned—I'm always like, Well, what have I *learned* from this situation?"). Here's what happened: She had scheduled a meeting with her boss, an executive, to discuss some logistical challenges on a show she was anchoring and how they might make some changes. A few minutes into the meeting, her boss said, out of the blue, "Well you know, everybody on the show hates you." Soledad basically just left the room and burst into tears.

"I was just completely blindsided," Soledad says. She called her husband, sobbing, and then called a good friend, a makeup artist who had a very Confucian way of thinking. Shockingly, her friend told her that the executive's statement was Soledad's own fault. "She told me, 'You have no one to blame but yourself. You went into that meeting unprepared.'" The friend explained that Soledad had allowed the executive to completely turn the tables on her. "I learned so much from that," she says. Now, if she goes into a meeting with an agenda (e.g., How do we fix the top part of the show?) and someone tries to shift the focus with completely unrelated feedback directed at her, she gets out her datebook and says, very nicely, something like, "You know, that's a really interesting idea. Why don't we set a meeting to talk about that—maybe next Tuesday at 8:30 A.M.? But right now I'd like to talk about what I came to discuss." It's a skillful and useful technique for "dodging" irrelevant and mean-spirited attacks that are couched as feedback.

Soledad's story about her boss's comment, in an almost ironic way, made me think of another Go-Getter Girl's philosophy regarding a reality of the workplace: office politics. How does a Go-Getter Girl deal with catty colleagues and the workplace rumor mill? Well, we know that Go-Getter Girls don't spend their days gossiping and whining. This is the work world, after all, not the middle-school cafeteria! Above, I spoke about Soledad's ability to tune out negativity on the job. For some Go-Getter Girls, dealing with the day-to-day challenge of navigating office politics means embracing a more self-preservationist mind-set.

Go-Getter Girl Melanie Parks* is an attractive, down-to-earth twenty-nine-year-old from New York. Through hard work and aggressive campaigning, Melanie managed to land an extremely glamorous job in advertising that, oh yeah, required her to move to Milan. There, she lived in a palatial apartment (which had been subsidized by her employer as a perk) that she couldn't invite her colleagues to, lest they wonder if she was getting paid triple their salaries. By the age of twenty-four she was fluent in Italian and had traveled all over the world for business and fun. A quick scan of her laptop photo album reveals shots in front of palaces in Moscow, on beaches in Cape Town, and at swanky hotels in Hong Kong.

Naturally, Melanie experienced a few "issues" with her colleagues at work. From early on in her career, Melanie had to deal with sabotage that was both subtle (catty e-mails) and blatant (the scheduling of meetings and business trips without her), from both female and male coworkers. One Thanksgiving break my friend Kristin* and I were visiting Melanie in her palatial Milan apartment, and Kristin and I were telling stories about a nemesis at work who took credit for a project ("Oh my gosh—I can't believe she *did* that!") and a boss who lied about giving a promotion. Melanie just smiled at us as if we were amateurs. "See, none of these things would bother you if you just remembered one simple thing," she sighed. Our ears perked up, eager for a prime nugget of GGG wisdom about to be imparted. "You have to remember that everybody at work hates you."

Huh? We said almost in unison. Excuse me? But I have *friends* at work—a real relationship and *mentorship* with my boss, I argued. "Maybe it seems that way," said Melanie. "But if you are in a competitive field, everyone hates you because you're just *more* and *better* than they think you should be: more attractive, more talented, smarter, whatever. They have to act like they like you, but they really hate you. Knowing this makes you successful because you won't forget that no one at work is your friend. Then you are not surprised when they try to play you."

Melanie's is a radical approach, indeed, and while it hasn't been my personal experience that my coworkers always *hate* me, in a big-picture sense, Melanie's point is well taken: in the business world, not everyone has your best interest in mind. You won't always understand the real motivation behind decisions coworkers and bosses make (why did *she* get promoted instead of me?), so you shouldn't get discouraged and lose sight of the big picture when you have minor defeats. Again, the philosophy may be extreme—but if there's a spectrum with opening up to and blindly trusting your coworkers at one end and with being more reserved and assuming that you have to watch your back at the other, leaning toward which end of that spectrum will serve you better? Probably the latter.

Think about the hit movie *Jerry Maguire*. It's one of my favorite movies, not necessarily for the now-clichéd "you complete me" denouement. I also liked the movie's keen, if fictionally flashy, insights on the competitive business of sports agents. The movie worked in part because it juxtaposed the romantic sentimentalities of man in love to the cold realities of man in work world, the latter of which is epitomized by Jerry's unceremonious firing at a crowded restaurant by his former friend and mentee—heck, his engagement-party organizer!—the sharklike Bob Sugar.

Jerry, if you'll recall, had written a mission statement on ethics for sports agents and for providing personal attention to clients, which he'd distributed to every employee at his agency's corporate conference. Despite the thunderous round of applause he initially received, you knew it was just a matter of time before he would be cut loose for veering from the agency's party line (i.e., more clients equals more money). As far as the overall moral of the story goes, the ambush-termination works out because, ultimately, Jerry does go on to greatness running his own shop based on his own fewer clients/more personal attention values. The movie, by the way, is based on the career of Leigh Steinberg, the preeminent sports agent and attorney who is known for his honesty and integrity and who only takes clients who are willing to give back to their communities.

While it's impossible to watch the movie without cringing at Bob Sugar's sneaky ways—and feeling sympathy for Jerry's mistreatment—the plotline hits the nail on the head of several key work-world realities that a Go-Getter Girl recognizes. First, it's quite possible that someone you trust will stab you in the back—and, obviously, this is all the more likely in cutthroat professions. This is not to say that you need to function every day out of paranoia, but, conversely, it's not particularly useful to walk around with grandiose notions that your boss, coworkers, or your company will always be loyal to you when their butt—or the bottom line—is in jeopardy. Instead, you should remain focused on your own career and simply be aware that your *main* focus should be "numero uno"—not what someone is doing in the cubicle next door.

Next—and this one is more difficult: when it comes to work, everybody is replaceable. In the movie, before Jerry leaves the office the day he is terminated, he delivers an inspired, three-minute monologue, to which everyone in the office gives their rapt attention. He goes on about how they should have treated him with manners and begs his former colleagues to come with him to his exciting new venture, an invitation that only the winning and idealistic Dorothy Boyd (played by Renée Zellweger) accepts. Then, on their triumphant exit, Jerry whispers to Dorothy, "Let's see how they do without us." Of course, approximately two seconds after they're gone, the office is up and running as fast as usual, all the worker bees buzzing and the agents yelling to the tunes of ringing phones and cell phones and to the zinging of copy and fax machines. Sure, there are loads of companies where the CEO or other top employees are integral to the company's success, but as a general guideline in managing your career, you will protect yourself from unnecessary hurt, and probably be more successful, if you focus on doing the very best that *you* can do each day—and have fewer expectations from your employer and coworkers. For example, don't expect warm and fuzzy treatment all the time. Don't take it personally or freak out when your boss takes two months to finally read the memo you slaved over for three weeks. Be annoyed, but not flabbergasted and bewildered, when a colleague lets you down or doesn't fulfill a promise. Then, as GGG Melanie said above, you'll be better able to take it in stride when you experience difficulties, or even some type of professional betrayal.

But what about navigating the office waters on a day-to-day basis? When it comes to dealing with the component of office politics you can control—in other words, your own behavior—try these key strategies:

Don't gossip, period! Whether you grew up with slam books or Facebook, we all know that gossiping with friends can be a harmless pastime, as long as it stays on the side of mildly catty/snarky, as opposed to downright vicious. But when it comes to work, gossiping can be a virtual career Charybdis that can send your productivity and prospects spiraling downward. First of all, it's a major distraction. Why does it really matter who got what assignment instead of you? Is it more useful to spend three hours kibbitzing about how Becky's mom knows the client or to take the same time to analyze your proposal and focus on what you could be doing to make sure you get the project next time? Second of all, constantly complaining and focusing on the negative will simply put you in a bad mood. Go-Getter Girls try their hardest to be upbeat and "glass half full" at work. Again, think, fake it till you make it. If you do find yourself unwittingly in a gossip situation—like, you're at lunch with some department peers and they all want to discuss your married boss's alleged affair—simply play dumb. Deflect with comments like "really?" or "huh, that can't be true!" Then, you're sort of participating in the conversation but not spreading or confirming any rumors. Think of yourself as a capsule of information—not a conduit for it. Now, let's say that you're caught between two dueling cliques of women that each love to gossip about the other group. Again, you want no part of this sorority-type behavior. If they keep trying to draw you into their mean-spirited camps, you may have to diplomatically declare your neutrality. Try to be very casual, instead of all righteous. Mean Girl A: "Oh my gosh, Susan and Liz are so dumb, that presentation was like a second-grade book report." You: "I can see what you're saying, but, you know, they're pretty cool and fun. I like working with them." Mean Girl B: "Tina and Lindsay are such snobs. Can you believe those obnoxious Gucci bags they have?" You: "Yeah, it's a bit much, but they mean well. I've never really had any problem with them." A few of those comments, and each side will quickly cross you off their recruitment list.

Make friends, not enemies. As we discussed earlier, sometimes not everyone at work will like you, for reasons that are beyond your control—but that doesn't mean you have to encourage it. Watching out for "number one" does not mean acting like a b★tch! Go-Getter Girls are self-aware and strategic, not selfish, spiteful, or sneaky. Be pleasant, generous, cheerful, classy, and collegial. Offer to help people. Get involved in department committees or your company's work-life balance or affinity groups. Attend happy hours. Participate in office outings. Need more ideas to make friends?

- **Smile!** Say hello and good morning. It's such a simple gesture, and it puts others at ease and lets them know that you're approachable.

- **Demonstrate interest.** Initiate non-work-related conversation. Talk about neutral topics like one's kids, dog, nephew's birthday party. Make an effort to socialize with your coworkers at least fifteen minutes every day.

- **Ask for advice.** Who doesn't love feeling like they're an expert or helpful? You can ask about something work-related or something (not too) personal, like where's a good place to get your hair cut. Asking someone's opinion is a great way to show that you're engaged in your work life and to break the ice.

- **Perform random acts of kindness.** Is your boss or colleague having a bad day? A simple gesture or invitation can show you care (e.g., "I'm going out to grab a coffee. Can I bring you back anything?").

Remember: all people need a little attention, respect, and care. And one of the best ways to minimize cattiness is to let people see your (obviously) cool, down-to-earth personality and hear about what's going on in your world. It's important to be (and be seen as) part of the team—not snobby or aloof! Plus, talking with colleagues in a more quasi-social setting is a good way to gather information about office dynamics and power players and to get a heads-up on opportunities or projects that are coming down the pipeline.

Find ways to self-promote, without looking opportunistic. Of course, one of the keys to getting ahead is making your superiors and coworkers aware of your ambition and accomplishments—but nobody likes a brownnoser! Thus, to avoid political snafus, your star moments need to be well considered—and context is key. For example, if you're assigned a particular, *individual* project—like delivering the monthly sales report, developing a new marketing strategy for a top client, or presenting a re-design for a publication—do everything you can to knock the final product out of the park. Be completely prepared, well researched, and succinct. Bring your A game to the point that *you* set the standard for what all future colleagues' presentations should be!

But let's say the same project is a *group* project. Do NOT actively try to show up everybody on the team by, say, secretly doing extra work or undermining your teammates' points during the actual presentation. That is not a good way to try to shine; it will make people resent you. Likewise, if you have a fabulous idea for a creative new initiative or project, set up a meeting with your boss to discuss your well-thought-out proposal, spreadsheets and all. Don't necessarily bring it up in the weekly department meeting where everyone perhaps goes around the room and talks about what he or she is working on. Why not? Because you'll find yourself talking to a room full of scowls and rolling eyes ("Why is she trying to make us all look bad?") from your peers—instead of having the rapt attention of the person who is the decision maker.

Vent to family and friends, not your cubicle mate. If you're blabbing about everything you hate about your job to coworkers, you do so at your own risk. As your parents might have said, you never know who's tak-ing your measure, and complaints often find their way to the ears of someone you wish they hadn't. One GGG CEO told me that whenever one of her employees complains about her to their managers—thinking she won't find out—within five minutes that manager has come to her office and told her exactly what the employee said. Sure, every now and then you'll need a couple of trusted colleagues to commiserate with about mundane grievances ("I can't believe we had to sit in that boring training for five hours!"). But for the really juicy stuff (e.g., "After what happened today, I'm *this close* to quitting!" or "My boss is a complete and total idiot!"), save it for your family and nonworkplace friends.

Remember: while you will develop genuine friendships and mentorships with coworkers, you must remain mindful that you are there—and getting paid—to do a job, not live out an episode of *The Hills*! This is business, after all. In general, Go-Getter Girls think in terms of *strategically* forging their own path, despite the climate of their work environment and what their coworkers are or are not doing.

Take the example of Go-Getter Girl Lizanne Falsetto, a former model and the founder of Think products, the multimillion-dollar business that makes all-natural energy bars with names like Think Green and Think Organic. Lizanne was nothing if not strategic from the advent of her modeling career. She'd wanted to be a model since she was five years old—"I put magazine photos all over my walls," she says—but coming from a strict Italian Catholic family, she was expected to get married and become a stay-at-home mom one day. When she was fourteen, she begged her parents to let her attend modeling classes. She convinced her dad to take her downtown to the John Powers modeling school each week, and he waited outside while she attended her two-hour classes.

Lizanne studied at Powers for two years then graduated from high school.

She was walking down the street in Seattle when—you know how the story goes—she was spotted by a Japanese modeling agent. He asked Lizanne whether she would like to go to Japan! A month later she was on a flight to Tokyo, embarking on what would be thirteen years of whirlwind travel, modeling throughout Asia, Europe, and the United States.

Lizanne loved modeling—everything from the smells of exotic cities to the different languages to the myriad styles of clothing and makeup. Yes, it was a glamorous, jet-set life, but like any work world, there were some harsh realities—and Lizanne soon confronted them. "It was an emotional roller coaster," she says. In particular, she struggled with the inherent and intense scrutiny of her physical appearance. She remembers being on a flight back to her agency, and she had a pimple. "I was in a complete panic, because when I got to the agency, I knew everyone would be looking at and analyzing the pimple!" she says. To Lizanne it was just a little blemish, and she'd wished everyone would just leave her alone. But to staff members at the agency, it wasn't that simple: they were all worried about losing the contract. This was business—and it was a business based on looks. Lizanne found that in a sea of exquisitely beautiful models, she was just "okay"—and she would need to do something different to succeed past them. This realization happened when, well, Lizanne stopped getting work!

GGG Nugget of Wisdom: *In any work situation, you must learn how to strategically assess the situation, discover and embrace your strengths and weaknesses, and convert constructive criticism into the fuel that powers your career forward.*

Though at first Lizanne cried a lot to "toughen herself" and develop what she calls a "heart of steel," she knew that to survive in modeling and succeed, she would need to run her career as a consummate, strategic professional. So, when every model was scrambling for jobs during the Paris fashion week, Lizanne would fly back to the States to score all the newly open gigs, which the top models had abandoned. When other girls were surviving on cigarettes, coffee, and alcohol—partly because they were trying to maintain weight and could never find any healthy food in the airports—Lizanne stuck to a diet of lean protein, fruits, veggies, no wheat ("It bloated me"), and no white sugar or white starches, which not only helped her maintain her weight but also gave her energy and vitality. She even started baking her own natural cookie bars to give her energy on the go, which (who knew?) would later become the prototypes for her postmodeling megabusiness. Finally, Lizanne discovered that having a "twinkle in her eye" and pleasant personality were to her competitive advantage. "I was never arrogant," she says. "People liked me for who I was."

This last realization occurred when Lizanne went to the casting for a huge advertising campaign for an airline, in which an American would be featured wearing a kimono for the first time, a huge honor in Japan. Lizanne stood in line for hours, wearing her ripped-up jeans, a T-shirt, a cowboy hat, and no makeup (as was typical of casting calls). When it was her turn to audition, the first thing the judges asked her and the other models to do was kneel, as one would in a religious temple. "And that was it!" Lizanne says. "They just said thank you, and we were told we could leave!" But Lizanne held back just a moment, and all the judges looked at her, and she looked at them and smiled. "In that moment, I was just thinking to myself, wouldn't that be cool to wear a kimono, which was such an honor in Japan. I was thankful for the opportunity to just be there."

For sure, something from Lizanne's inner spirit must have affected the company, because the next day her agent called to tell her she got the big campaign! She was on practically every billboard and poster all over Tokyo, in an ad that represented Asia inviting foreigners to visit the Asian world. What sold the casting agents? Lizanne thinks that during that brief moment when she looked back, the eye contact between her and the judges revealed her honesty and depth: "They could see that I knew and believed in what an honor it was to wear the kimono in that campaign."

Almost ironically in a profession that seemed so focused on outward beauty, Lizanne's inner beauty and strength won her the job—at least that day! Sure, it's a bit of a touchy-feely story, but I couldn't help thinking that it was perhaps a metaphor for the Go-Getter Girl spirit—because not only do Go-Getter Girls like Lizanne radiate inner confidence, but having it and depending on it is what helps them navigate and advance their careers. You too can and must tap into your own inner confidence to help guide your career. If you're not feeling so confident, how can you begin to build up your self-esteem? Try these tips for getting a little GGG boost:

- Make a goal, however small (e.g., painting the bathroom), and accomplish it.

- Sign up for a physically challenging "powergirl" activity, like Tae Kwon Do classes.

- Enroll in an acting or public-speaking class like Toastmasters.

- Buy a book on affirmations. Say them to yourself daily. Heck, read them twenty times a day if you need to. Stick a secret Post-It with your own personal "Go me!" message in your desk drawer.

- Write a glowing bio of yourself. You've accomplished a lot! Make sure to include lots of references to all your great hidden talents, like having a penchant for buying great holiday gifts.

- Do something you think is a little scary, whether it's hiking on a local mountain or just baking a pie from scratch.

- Do some volunteer work.

The reality is that throughout the journey of your professional life, there will be jobs you won't get and projects that flounder. You will inevitably encounter challenges—and you may, very often, fail. *Every* one of the dozens of women I spoke to for this book failed multiple times—some were minor missteps, some were colossal catastrophes—but they all were able to tap into an inner strength to keep moving forward. Part of this process involves maintaining a laser-like focus on your goals. To help you get started, try the following exercise:

One of the keys to not sweating the small stuff at work is focus, focus, focus. While competitiveness is good, at some point you have to tune out what everyone else is doing and be more or less "inner-directed" to achieve your goals. So it's important to concretize those goals—whether that means becoming the youngest person to ever get promoted to manager in your department or simply showing up on time every day. Write down five things—doesn't matter how small—that you want to accomplish in your job:

1. _____

2. _____

3. _____

4. _____

5. _____

After all this talk about confidence, we can't leave this chapter without one final note: try your hardest not to cry at work. At the very least, do not do it in the presence of others: excuse yourself from the meeting, shut your office door, or exit the building. But sometimes sh*t happens. If you lose it one time, and suddenly visible tears are flowing in public, don't obsess over it. Pretend it never happened and try not to do it again. Just pick yourself up and move on. You're human! As with anything, GGGs realize that it's better to regroup and restrategize than to dwell on negative things that happen in the work world. Sure, in an ideal world we would never feel overwhelmed, we would always be praised for all the work we do, and we would be constantly inundated with job offers and promotions. But the reality is that the business world can be a tough, competitive place, populated by mean bosses and catty colleagues. This reality does not have to thwart your Go-Getter Girl spirit. Remember, by drawing on your inner strength and staying focused on your goals, you will survive—and thrive on the path to success!

3.

Expand Your Circle

*Y*ou know the saying "Good luck happens when preparedness meets opportunity"? Well, those words certainly ring true for Tamar Geller, the renowned dog trainer and bestselling author of *The Loved Dog*. Tamar grew up in Israel and served as an intelligence officer working with the Special Forces in the Israeli army, where she observed training techniques for aggressive dogs. In addition, she spent a few months in the Israeli desert studying the behavior of wolves as part of a research project. After her time in the military, and after traveling the globe for a few months, Tamar found herself in California for several weeks. Always a keen observer of animal behavior and determined not to just spend her days lying on the beach working on her tan, she decided to visit two dog trainers at a small agency, to ask them about their life's work. "I had absolutely no professional experience as a dog trainer—but during the conversation they told me about this client who was having a problem with his cocker spaniel who kept stealing his socks," she says. "They eventually asked me to go over and try out my techniques—because they didn't know what do!" Convinced that the dog was stealing the socks as a way to get attention, Tamar showed the owner how to ignore wrong behavior but give the dog plenty of playtime as well as positive feedback for proper behavior—and the dog stopped stealing the socks. And who was the dog's owner? The then almost-famous saxophonist Kenny G.

Kenny G., so happy that his dog's problem was solved, referred Tamar to a few of his friends, like Goldie Hawn, Whoopi Goldberg, and Nicollette Sheridan. "I was from Israel—so I didn't even really know that these people were 'celebrities,'" Tamar says. Soon, her loving and effective techniques with canines, which were founded on her belief that dogs needed to be trained in a fun and humane way, as the wolves she'd observed did with their young, spread through Hollywood and beyond, and client after client followed. Then, a few years ago, she was training Nicollette's golden retriever puppy, Oliver, on the set of the TV show *Desperate Housewives* when—lo and behold—Oprah Winfrey walked by. "Oprah saw the puppy there with the best manners. She was like, 'Oh, I want a puppy like that—and I want that woman to train him!'" A few weeks later, Tamar was being flown to Oprah's Chicago home to train the talk-show host's three new dogs. Now, several years and a whole lot of clients later, she has built a virtual dog-training empire with books, DVDs, television appearances, a doggy day care, doggie treats, doggie toys and products, and philanthropic initiatives.

One of the secrets of Tamar's success? Constantly expanding her circle—a key Go-Getter Girl activity—which Tamar sees as a way she's created her own luck. Tamar says that whenever opportunities came along to meet people, travel, or try new things, she took them. "I wasn't the type to say, 'Oh no, this doesn't fit into my schedule,'" she says. In particular, she constantly was reaching out to new people and seeking new experiences that fell outside her comfort zones. "I could barely speak English, and in my mind, I had no idea what I was doing being a dog trainer! But you have to push through your comfort zone," she says. "I think a lot of people aren't comfortable with being uncomfortable."

In the process, Tamar found herself in the presence of many people who could introduce her to *other* people who would move her career forward. In his bestselling book *The Tipping Point* (Back Bay Books, 2002), Malcolm Gladwell posits the theory that such people are "connectors": people who innately or purposefully have a huge circle of friends and, more important, acquaintances, and have a distinct talent for "bringing the world together." As a Go-Getter Girl, you either are a connector or you need connectors in your life, pronto! The idea is not necessarily to "handpick" your contacts. If anything, you want to indiscriminately expand your social and professional circles, gathering acquaintances from different backgrounds, social circles, and professional spheres. Immersing yourself in new experiences that place you in diverse situations is the best way to do this. After all, networking is about getting outside yourself, and you don't want to limit your connectivity. You never know who knows who, and the contact of your dreams might just show up at an unexpected place or time. Who knew Oprah would be walking by that *Desperate Housewives* set at exactly the time Tamar was training one of her client's dogs?

GGG Nugget of Wisdom: *As they say, 80 percent of success is just showing up. Make it your mission to (almost always) show up, even when you don't feel like it—whether it's to a professional or social event. You never know who you'll meet and, more important, you'll probably have fun!*

Throughout your career, you need to take note of people who are connectors, like GGG Isabel González, a senior editor at *InStyle* and the former editor-in-chief of Hearst's *Tu Vida*, TV personality, and coauthor of the popular lifestyle and cookbook *Latin Chic*. Isabel is truly one of those gals who knows everyone. She has friends and contacts from all backgrounds and is constantly expanding her circle. For Isabel, reaching out and being social is genuine and comes naturally, though she says that her connector status has deeper roots in her experiences growing up as what she calls an "outsider." Says Isabel, "I was the only Hispanic in my high school in Atlanta. My last name was weird. I was tall and skinny and wore glasses. I was never one of the popular kids. I felt marginalized." But this experience gave her a great vantage point to observe *other* people's social interactions. "Even though I wasn't part of those interactions, I intuitively came to know how and where connections were made—and that sometimes, when you put A and B together—if, say, A wants to write a play, and B knows a contact who is buying plays—then magic can happen."

In addition, having been raised by immigrant parents, whose success she says depended on people opening doors for them, Isabel is passionate about lending a hand to others trying to reach their dreams. While, like any successful professional, she uses discretion in sharing her Rolodex, she's more than willing to help someone when he or she shows talent and drive. "Our successes are not because of isolated instances," she says. "We don't operate in a bubble. Everyone needs to seek out resources and support to get to the next level."

These points are illustrated by the typical way that Isabel reaches out to draw people into her life: Referred by a mutual acquaintance, Isabel sent me an e-mail to promote her upcoming book. We chatted over e-mail and hit it off, and I ended up pitching and interviewing Isabel for an article in *Atlanta* magazine about her book. Several months later, when I was in New York for a television appearance, I met with my friend Beth Parker,★ who was trying to break into the New York magazine business as an art director. Thinking it couldn't hurt to ask, I e-mailed Isabel (whom I really didn't "know" very well but for our few e-mails and interview) to ask if she might, by chance, be willing to introduce Beth to some folks at *Teen People*, where Isabel was an editor. Isabel agreed and soon discovered that she and Beth had gone to the same high school in Georgia! When Beth arrived at Isabel's office in Manhattan, Isabel welcomed her with open arms and introduced her to everyone at the magazine. Soon afterward, those people put Beth in touch with just about everyone who's anyone in the New York design world, and within six months Beth had landed a plum gig at a highly respected women's magazine—no doubt because of superconnector Isabel!

And Beth didn't stop her "connecting" there. Once in New York, she continued to follow up and reach out to all those creative directors whom she met during her "exploratory" phase, connections that continued to come in handy down the road. For example, a few years later she got a call from the creative director at a big-name magazine, whom she'd met years earlier, about a job opportunity there. And, after one of Beth's bosses moved on to another publication and had an opening, he called Beth to come be his deputy. Publishing—like many other professions—is a small world, and often, getting a job is all about who you know. Case in point: despite the fact that she has interviewed with human-resource departments at all the big publishing houses, Beth says, "Not one of the actual jobs I got came from those HR interviews." Rather, she has always gotten jobs from personal contacts she made at an actual publication.

Stories like Beth's illustrate just how important it is to expand your inner circle when you are looking for a job outside your company, but it might surprise you that sometimes advancement requires you to be just as proactive about connecting with others *inside* your workplace. Even—and particularly—if you are a self-proclaimed introvert or very shy. Consider the example of *Washington Post* advice columnist Carolyn Hax, who swears that she is "not a networker in any way."

Carolyn, who has written the "Tell Me About It" column in the *Post* since 1997, got into newspapers out of sheer desperation. After graduating from Harvard with a degree in History and Literature, she considered grad school and law school but dismissed both after (1) realizing she didn't like being a student and (2) undertaking a stint as a paralegal that proved to her that law wasn't her natural place. At this point, Carolyn needed a job, so she thought, "Well, I could be a journalist!" Carolyn started out as an associate editor at the *Army Times*, where she worked for two years. Then, after several interviews, one failed copy test (which they let her retake), and literally an entire summer of proofing and rewriting *Post* articles, Carolyn landed a job as a copy editor at the *Washington Post*.

Like most jobs, the copy-editor position had good and bad aspects to it. On the one hand, it was a great opportunity and learning experience; it was fast paced and adrenaline-rush scary, in a good way. "There were such consequences to your work," Carolyn says. "You get something wrong, and there it is in the paper!" Fortunately, there were many seasoned editors reading behind her (she was on what is called the "rim" and was the first read on articles; usually there were two other edits after hers to catch all the things that she missed). But on the other hand, Carolyn found it to be kind of an isolated, "dark and headachy" experience. After their big deadline push each day, there would be silence and quiet proofreading all night; unbeknownst to Carolyn, she had vision problems and would get headaches reading night after night after night. "So maybe it wasn't the happiest years of my life, but overall it was still good. I liked the people, and they liked me and liked my work enough that I didn't feel like I was constantly hanging on [for my life]," she says.

But looking around, Carolyn figured out pretty quickly that she couldn't be a copy editor forever because she didn't have enough of a hawk eye for subtle grammatical errors and didn't have the desire to one day lead the desk, and at the *Post*, you "write or you die." "That's the typical path to 'advancement,'" Carolyn says, noting that most of the paper's top editors "wrote their way into those positions." By this point, Carolyn had been promoted a few times and was now a news editor, clearing pages for print. "But there was something about going into work at night, doing something that I had hoped was leading to something else, that made it not sit right with me," she says. In short, she wanted more—but how to get there?

Carolyn knew innately that she needed to "make some noise"—to reach out in order to get noticed. "The first thing I did was talk to my editor in the 'Style' section, Mary Hadar, and say I have all this ambition and no place to put it," Carolyn says. Mary told Carolyn she would need to write some free-lance pieces in order to build clips and gave her some advice on how to think of ideas. "That was actually my biggest problem: coming up with ideas. I could write all day if you pointed me in the right direction. But going out in the world looking for ideas, I don't have the reporter's eye for a great story," Carolyn says. Later on, after she'd freelanced a few small lifestyle pieces—and not particularly enjoying it or having "much impact"—she ended up having a meeting with Len Downie and Bob Kaiser, who were then executive editor and managing editor of the *Post*. "At this point, I was really ready to tell anybody that I wanted more." Len and Bob told her to go see Kate Boo, at that time an editor of the "Outlook" opinion section. Carolyn walked right over and introduced herself. They talked about what kind of stories Carolyn could do, and she ended up writing a few pieces for "Outlook" about things that, as Carolyn says, got her "all fired up."

GGG Nugget of Wisdom: *In work and in life, getting what you want often requires reaching outside of your comfort zone.*

Carolyn recalls that during this time period her job wasn't all bad, but because she so firmly saw herself as temporary in the copyediting world, moving forward was always in the forefront of her mind. "I was searching. I wanted to know how to advance when I had gotten onto this path, and I looked around me and there were no bridges. There were just none. And so that was my question, How do I get from here to there—to the other side of the chasm?" she says. Instead of racking her own brain with this question, Carolyn started asking anyone and everyone in the newsroom who would sit down with her. Her modus operandi would go something like this: "Someone would tell me go talk to so-and-so, and I would go knock on their door (this was back before e-mail) and say, 'Um, excuse me, do you have a minute?' [waving her hand], and I would falter my way to asking, 'How do you get from point A to point B when there are no bridges?'"

Carolyn says that of course she was scared to approach these big-name writers and editors—but she literally forced herself to spit the words out. "I'm a big stammerer and finder of words and false starter and sufferer of dry mouth!" she jokes. "I'd be 'like, um, okay [deep breath], um, I was talking to Bob and Len and they said I should talk to you [sigh, whew!].'" Carolyn points out that these impromptu meetings were the *opposite* of "let's go out to lunch and talk about my future." Rather, this was someone telling her, point-blank, you don't have this credential, which means you need to go get X, Y, and Z. "I would literally say to them, 'I have more ambition than I have qualifications—so how do we fix this?' They'd tell me what to do, and I'd say thank you." Usually, the conversations lasted all of five minutes! But at the end of the day, she got out of her comfort zone and got to know tons of people in the newsroom. She was expanding her network, putting herself in the right place at the right time—priming herself for just the perfect opportunity to come along.

Fast-forward some months, and Carolyn, to her surprise, ascended to advice columnist. As part of her regular job, she ended up working with the editor of the "Style Plus" section, Peggy Hackman, on special projects–type work. One day they were talking, and Carolyn learned that Peggy was being asked to take on an existing teenage advice column. Carolyn knew the *Post* was concerned about having more features for younger readers and that this particular advice column was currently being written by somebody in her eighties. "I just said to Peggy, 'These columns are all tired—what they really need is a snotty thirty-year-old writing them!'" Carolyn had turned thirty about two months earlier, and something in her mind just sort of clicked. But at that moment, she didn't say anything about it. "Then the next day I went back to her and said, 'You know how we were talking about advice columns yesterday? It's sort of stuck with me.' I told her, 'I think we can do it.'" Carolyn took a handful of the column's questions and answered them—typed her responses and printed them out on the regular office printer. Carolyn gave them to Peggy, who took a look and ended up circulating the sample to Downie, Hadar, and the top editors, who all loved them. "Just six or seven weeks later, all of a sudden, I'm this news editor-slash-columnist!"

If she hadn't expanded her network inside the *Post* and actively sought out new opportunities, would Carolyn have stumbled on what became her dream job? Who can say? But the process of reaching out to get there had value in itself: Carolyn felt better knowing that she was taking control—of her own actions—by at least trying to find a niche that fit. In a way, she had no choice. "What was I going to do? I had to do *something* to get out of my rut!" she says. And when she did, it was a breakthrough. Writing the sample columns felt so easy and natural. "If you could put hand gestures into your writing, that's how I felt!" The words just flowed onto the page—no obsessing or agonizing back and forth as she had done with all her copyediting or previous freelance projects. Even though for a few years, until the column became full-time, she was straddling the two sides—copy editor and columnist—she immediately felt renewed and excited. "I had gotten a solid footing on the side that I wanted to be on, the side of [something unique and interesting] that had some sort of future for me," she says. And, as a true Go-Getter Girl, Carolyn had made that opportunity happen for herself.

GGG Nugget of Wisdom: *Expanding your network is not about having expectations. It's about making yourself open and available for new opportunities—and the possibility that you will be inspired to take an exciting new path.*

If, even after hearing these Go-Getter Girls' stories, you still think that they just got "lucky" and that "getting out there" can only lead to pithy advice or a stack of fancy business cards, you may need a paradigm shift. Social scientists, such as Meredith Rolfe, a political sociologist at Oxford, have argued that our connections with *loose* acquaintances, or "weak ties"—instead of close friends, family, or strongly connected business associates—are the most helpful thing in the quest for professional or financial success. In particular, the more varied the ties, the better: "In access to information, the volume of ties is less important than the diversity of those ties," Rolfe explained in "The Laws of Urban Energy," an article in *Psychology Today* (Jul/Aug 2007). "A smaller number of ties which lead off to different types of information would be more useful than a larger number of ties with redundant paths to the same information" (e.g., think of having lots of contacts in different departments of your company, not just your own department, and in various industries, not just your own profession).

Moreover, the personal benefits of these interactions range from increased creativity to the intellectual benefits of diversity to simple feelings of security and satisfaction with your environment. In other words, taking the initiative to connect can simply lift your spirits, as it did for Carolyn. For example, GGG Sarah Sands,★ age twenty-eight and a publicist for high-powered K Street clients in Washington, D.C., found that even brief connections during regular runs have the power to perk up her day. When she previously lived in Atlanta, she observed that fellow runners would always smile and wave and say hello, making a tiny bit of chitchat on their routes. In D.C., jogging was a slightly different scene, with runners she saw tending to be blinders-on, head-straight-forward, no interaction whatsoever. "It was so sad!" says Sarah. At first, Sarah followed the status quo but soon found it too depressing. "Now I go on these runs on the Rock Creek trails, and I'm like, 'Hi, how are you? Have a great day!' as I run by. They probably think I'm nuts, but it makes me happy!" she says.

Sarah has always been someone to make connections without really even trying—just by talking to people as she goes about her day-to-day life, whether she's at a restaurant or the post office. And very often these impromptu meetings end up being good for her professional life. Recently, for example, she met a woman at her gym who, it turned out, works at an important government agency. "We just got to talking because I told her I liked her T-shirt, and she knew I was training for a marathon and asked how it was going. We were talking about work, and then all of a sudden we realized we both do the same thing, and that she might be a new client—so we set up a dinner," Sarah says, noting that she always thinks it's silly when employees (or their bosses) think that it's useful to just sit in your office all day, every day. "That's not where the business comes," she says. "The business is *outside*! It's about making connections."

Again, the point is not that you constantly need to be "networking" in order to be successful! (There are times for more "conscious" connecting—and we'll talk about those in the next chapter.) The point here is simply that expanding your network—getting out there and connecting, experiencing and *enjoying* life—will have social and professional benefits. If you feel like you're in a rut, is it really going to help if you sit in your house every night, pouting, and, say, watching TiVoed marathons of your favorite shows? Yes, there's a (finite) time and a place for this activity (hello, *Project Runway*!), but sometimes you just need to get up and out of the house! To help you get started, here are a few little tips:

Lower your expectations. Don't think you have to go to some networking event and gather thirty business cards! That idea is

GGG PEARL:
On Business Cards

Have them handy to give out. Ask for others' cards, with utmost discretion (e.g., don't bombard a superstar). If you don't have them from your job, order them online. Choose a nice, thick card stock, not too glossy. If you're listing a personal e-mail address, make sure it's a simple one (pam .smith@gmail.com) not a silly one (diva girl52@gmail.com).

not only overwhelming—but it's also not particularly useful. Think baby steps. Some naturally shy Go-Getter Girls consciously tell themselves, "I'll just go, and play it by ear." Have a drink. Engage, or just stand on the side and observe. Just show up, for practice.

Keep an open mind. Ditch all latent snobbiness or cynicism when it comes to trying new things. Asked to attend a party with a new crowd? Invited to a restaurant featuring cuisine you don't normally eat? Your best friend wants to go to body boot camp this Saturday, but you're more of a yoga girl? When it comes to a situation that is "different," just try it—at least once! That's the attitude of GGG Kate Edwards, the thirty-something U.S. CEO of Jentro, a German navigation-software company. Kate says that there's nothing she's not been curious about—whether it's hiking, sailing, painting, or getting a big tattoo. To conquer her fear of "running into Jaws" in the ocean, she even forced herself to learn scuba diving, and not just anywhere: at the famous Blue Hole in Belize, where (nonthreatening) sharks regularly swim. She says that whenever she tries something outside "core experience," she not only learns from the experience and often discovers how much she loves the new activity but also uses the information in other situations. "Every little experience I have somehow gets incorporated into some other aspect of my life," Kate says. That applies whether it's knowing how to stand when the wind gusts in Chicago because of her experiences sailing or thinking more creatively from hanging out with her artist friends in contrast to the analytically minded folks she works with in finance and technology.

Participate in extracurricular activities. It may seem like common sense, but to make connections, you need to put yourself in a place where people congregate! According to "The Laws of Urban Energy," the previously mentioned article in *Psychology Today,* diverse social contact can stimulate your creativity and promote innovative thinking. Plus, it can be a great way to meet new friends. You can try joining a gym, book club, cultural association, volleyball league, church or synagogue; getting a hobby or taking a class in cooking, dance, jewelry making, or creative writing; or even frequenting the same coffee shop. I remember when I was preparing for the bar exam, I studied at a neighborhood Starbucks every day for hours. There was another girl there at the same time as I was every day who was obviously studying for the bar, too— she had a stack of review guides called *BAR BRI* that are a dead give- away! Eventually the girl asked, "So, which bar are you taking?" We introduced ourselves—her name was Maria—and soon discovered we had shared friends from law school, would be working at similar firms, and simply had a lot in common. Sure, from that point on, we wasted a little time just talking and commiserating every other day instead of studying, but our chitchat sure made the study process less dreary—and I had made my first new friend in D.C.

Pretend you're a reporter, but not in an obnoxious way. You know those girls who just seem to start up a conversation with anybody and every- body, no matter what the situation? My best friend Amina is just like that. We'll be at Loehmann's, for example, and she'll see a girl trying on the same chic sandals as her and say, "These are so cute! For just twenty bucks, aren't they a steal?," and two minutes later they're in a deep conversation about the differences between American and Puerto Rican fashion, which, Amina apparently learned, is where the young woman is from and will be visiting next week. Well, if you're shy, one trick to "getting out there" is to have the mind-set that you have a professional *purpose* in exploring. For example, think like you're a reporter—and you're getting out there for "research" purposes, scouting out a new shop or restaurant or striking up a conversation with a random person to get information for your story. Just don't go overboard and be obnoxious about it by asking a zillion hard-nosed questions!

If you try to expand your mind and your network for the possibility of new and amazing opportunities, soon you'll be making new connections at every turn. So get out there and begin to knock on some doors, literally or figuratively! Eventually, just like the Go-Getter Girls in this chapter, one of those doors will open to a once-in-a-lifetime opportunity.

How to Schmooze

*L*et's start from the basic idea that "schmoozing"—even by people who look like they are completely natural charmers—does not happen by accident. Whether you're a "superconnector" like Isabel Gonzáles, from the previous chapter, or a little less outgoing, there are some techniques you can learn so that you too can light up the room with your sparkling smile and wit! Now, you may feel put off by the notion of conscious schmoozing. But from a practical perspective, you will likely find yourself in a situation that requires a little forced networking, such as a re-cruiting event, work dinner, or even dinner with your boyfriend's parents, at some point in your life. Why not be prepared? Here are some insights from Go-Getter Girls who've got great schmoozing know-how.

Go-Getter Girl Jen Bluestein has worked in politics long enough that she has no trouble instantly getting "on message." She's built an exciting career from serving as a press secretary for New York City Public Schools to working on the campaigns of the mayor of Newark, Cory Booker, and the New York City mayoral candidate, Fernando Ferrer, to consulting for Bono of U2's DATA (debt, AIDS, trade, Africa) organization to undertaking her current role heading up Teach for America's Political Leadership Initiative—all jobs that involve talking to lots of people about lots of pointed issues all day long. "It's my job to be able to handle the 'one-pager' that explains my project," she says.

As part of her work, Jen often finds herself at fund-raisers, parties, and events where it's important for her to make a connection—but, when it comes to how she does so, Jen tries to do anything but deliver a rote script about herself or her organization. Instead, she asks as many questions as she can.

The reasons behind her technique are threefold: First, Jen has found that if you start talking, you lose people really quickly: "Even if they like what you're talking about—and they file it away and plan to go home and Google it—they still think, 'This girl was *pitching* me,'" Jen says, "and, they either think, 'She's pitching and that's it' or, even worse, they think, 'She's ultimately *serving herself* because she's pitching.'" Second, Jen doesn't talk about herself because she won't learn anything! "I already know what my project is—so I don't need to be talking to myself about it!" she says. "If I have five minutes with someone new I meet, the better use of time is to listen to them and figure out what's going on with them and what their interest level is, what their knowledge level is, what moves them, what inspires them . . . , who they are," Jen says. Then, she can end the conversation on an uptick, saying something like, "I'm really glad you're looking into this. Our team will be in touch."

When she does follow up or see them again, she actually has more to go on because she got to know them in a more sincere way. For example, Jen will often "close the loop," as she says, on a meaningful connection she's made by sending an e-mail the next day or so to her new acquaintance. She might include something like "Last night you mentioned that you had been involved in a report about X" or "You mentioned this program you saw on *60 Minutes*" or "I really liked learning about your trip to Italy." Says Jen, "I've gathered enough information that the e-mail can be honest and genuine—and you have so much more to describe your interaction." This deeper level of understanding is particularly important in the work that Jen currently does, which, in part, involves encouraging Teach for America alumni to run for office one day, a desire that may take months or years to cultivate.

GGG Nugget of Wisdom: *Sometimes small talk is just that; it won't or doesn't need to lead to anything more. But think of it sometimes as an opportunity to plant the seeds to cultivate a new social relationship over time.*

Finally, the third reason Jen focuses on asking questions instead of talking is—as any basic networking book will tell you—that people love to talk about themselves! "They get psyched!" she says. And, ironically enough, people actually come away from the interaction with a more favorable impression of you.

As we saw from Jen's MO, once the ice has been broken, asking questions is a fabulous technique to build rapport—but what if it's difficult for you to even work up the courage to get a conversation started with someone you don't know? Consider the "schmooze mind-set" strategy of GGG Regina

Smith,* age thirty-six and originally from Kansas City. When Regina became the editor of an award-winning arts and entertainment magazine in Phoenix, she wasn't worried about her cover lines and newsstand sales. She was, instead, concerned about one of the seemingly fun parts of her new job: schmoozing. Making the local rounds with the city's cognoscenti may have seemed glamorous to some, but to Regina it was a pain in the neck. She was naturally introverted and, like many editors, had a razor-sharp bullsh*t detector, so striking up conversations and name-dropping with total strangers (many of whom, let's face it, tended to be of the vapid variety) was a burden. "I didn't like it," she says, "but I had to do it because it was part of the job." So Regina devised a plan to break her introvert inclinations. She would tell herself before each event that she would talk to just three or four new people. She would take a deep breath, put on the schmooze smile, approach a new person, and "turn it on"—but only for limited periods of time. "Then, after I'd done my schmooze duty for the night, I could sit back and just *relax*," she says, breathing an almost audible sigh of relief as she recalls the thought of retiring from working a room of strangers.

Regina's story reveals that schmoozing can be strategized, even if you are not naturally outgoing or chatty. And while it's great to have a method for how to schmooze, Go-Getter Girls understand that it's equally important to know the rules of how not to schmooze. If you are in a professional situation— for example, a work-related dinner, cocktail party, or sporting event—you are always "on," and you should never just "wing" it. Consider the example of Brianna Sutherland,* age twenty-six, a summer associate at a big, swanky law firm in Chicago. These law-firm summer programs are notorious schmooze fests, packed to the brim with lunches, dinners, golfing events, baseball games, zoo outings, and any number of other uncomfortable, contrived situations where the summers, as they are called, are expected to "get to know" one another and the firm's attorneys. Ask any lawyer who's been through this sugarcoated hazing ritual and they will recall the experience with an ugh and a cringe. In a sick Machiavellian twist, it's common for attorneys to bait the competing summers with questions about what they "hate" about the job or overly personal questions, just to see if the kiddos fall for the trap. Of course, a GGG would know that saying less is more and would avoid accidentally sticking her foot in her mouth at the first schmooze opportunity.

Brianna, however, did just that. During the first week of work, at a lunch attended by Brianna, other summers, and a high-powered partner, Brianna—an all-around nice, smart, and talented girl—got a bit nervous and attempted to fill the awkward silences with "small talk." By the end of the first course, she had told the whole table that she and her boyfriend had reached a critical turning point in their relationship the previous year. After breaking up because he couldn't commit, they had recently reconciled and now were constantly bickering over the division of labor in the household. Things had apparently gotten better now that her boyfriend had decided to take over dishes duty, but it was still really difficult because, as a history professor, he had a lot less job security than she did. She continued in this vein for a good twenty minutes, desperate to keep the conversation going.

No, no, no! I wanted to shout. There were so many things wrong with this "schmooze attempt"—from the timing (just one week on the job!) to the situation (a lunch with *many* colleagues) to the content (which was *way* too personal, demonstrated qualities that might not be advantageous in a competitive work environment, and undermined her level of responsibility and dependability).

Of course, midway through this unfortunate case of "TMI," the partner was rolling her eyes and making eyes at the other summers at the table with a look that said, What is this girl talking about? For the rest of the summer, Brianna was known as someone who was perhaps emotionally unstable and, at the very least, had difficulty separating work from personal life. This TMI reputation stayed with her in many people's view at the firm, which was unfortunate because she really was an extremely bright and competent future attorney.

Brianna's story illustrates the potential pitfalls of sharing too much information about one's personal life at work. Think about it: doesn't it make you slightly uncomfortable when you hear colleagues at work-related events make conversation about how they can't pay their rent or, even worse, say bad things about their significant others or families? This type of talk not only is inappropriate, unnecessary, and borderline tacky but also can leave lasting impressions that inevitably affect how colleagues perceive your abilities as an employee. You must have some boundaries; thus, it is critical for GGGs to stay up on current events and pop culture

GGG PEARL:
On Being a Media Maven

To become a stimulating conversationalist, you've got to have some interesting things to talk about—besides your charming self! Find great stories or pop-culture currency to share at your next cocktail party by consuming a bit of the following:

- NPR
- *60 Minutes*
- morning television programs (e.g., *Today Show, Squawk Box, American Morning*)
- *The Wall Street Journal*
- *The New York Times*, Sunday edition
- *Women's Health, Self, US Weekly, Fast Company,* or *National Geographic* magazines
- *Esquire* or *Men's Journal* magazines (yes, men's magazines often have fantastic, universally appealing feature stories!)

and to talk about things *outside* themselves in order to steer clear of an accidental "diarrhea of the mouth" episode! So what are some good topics for small talk?

- current movies, books, and plays
- television programs or magazine and newspaper articles
- new restaurants
- recent or upcoming vacations
- sports
- celebrity gossip (in moderation)
- the weather

Yes, some of these subjects may seem a little silly and mundane, but small talk is often just about making polite conversation. (On that note, it's generally inadvisable to delve into race, religion, or politics—but consider your context. Obviously, if you're at a political fund-raiser, politics is likely to come up! Even then, err on the side of less is more and always be tactful.)

Now, what about the logistics of the actual schmooze convo? Consider having something in your hand, like your drink or your clutch bag. It gives you something to hold and thus minimizes nervous fidgeting. Then, there's the opening. Whether you're standing around waiting to be approached or (Oh geez! Deep breath . . .) you're the person talk-

- HBO *Real Sports* (same reasoning as above)
- "Page Six"
- Salon and Slate.com
- any book on the bestseller lists

ing first, open with a genuine compliment (what woman doesn't like to hear she has nice shoes?) or mention the food or the surroundings ("Isn't the chicken satay fantastic?" or "What a beautiful view!"). Introduce yourself. Make eye contact. Engage in some small talk (see above). If you find that you have stuff in common, just go with the flow and converse (you know how)! Ask questions that you are genuinely curious about—and listen. If someone you know walks over to join in, introduce the two with an engaging detail ("Oh, hi, Jim!" To Sue: "Jim works with me in marketing." To Jim: "Sue was just telling me about her trip to Spain!"). Then, when the conversation sail loses its wind—or maybe even a little before that point, just to keep the energy flowing—make a graceful exit. For example, you might pull over and introduce another acquaintance while you walk away (e.g., "Oh, Val, you have to meet Becky! I must go grab those hors d'oeuvres now!). Or to keep it simple, a very breezy, "I think I'll go grab a drink" or "It was so nice chatting with you—I hope we bump into each other again soon!" usually does the trick.

Wasn't that easy and painless? Okay, it can be a lot harder in person—but one way to get over the fear is to prepare even more. Devise your own Schmooze Action Plan, as follows:

As you know, Go-Getter Girls try to show up, literally and figuratively, for social- and career-networking opportunities. When you're about to enter a new social environment, the pressure to mindlessly mingle can create anxiety, so consider creating a Schmooze Action Plan. Having minigoals for talking to new people will help you break free from "wallflower" mode and make the process less intimidating. You can tell yourself, "I just have to talk to one more new person, and then I can be introverted for a while!" Remember, strategic schmoozing involves more than just getting someone's business card and, ironically, the more you let people talk about themselves, the more favorable impression they will have of you. So before going to your next event, write down the following:

Three specific people or types of people I want to speak to:

1. _____

2. _____

3. _____

Three questions to ask each:

1. _____

2. _____

3. _____

1. _____

2. _____

3. _____

1. _____

2. _____

3. _____

Three current event "nuggets" to discuss:

1. _____

2. _____

3. _____

Finally, if you've made a connection with someone, make sure to follow up within a few days and express how much you enjoyed speaking with them.

Now that you've got some useful tools, I hope that you can see that schmoozing can actually be easy, productive—and fun! Just give it a try. And one final little point—when in doubt, just smile a lot and be your cute self. Smiling puts people at ease. Eventually, someone will come over and say hello— heck, maybe even a cute guy, which is never a bad thing!

Part Two

LOOK GOOD
WHILE
YOU'RE AT IT

5.

Maintain a
Healthy Lifestyle

*G*o-Getter Girls come in all shapes and sizes, but whether they are thin, curvy, or full figured, they pride themselves on being fit. The same discipline it takes to rapidly achieve education and career goals is manifest in the fact that GGGs find a healthy eating and fitness plan that works for them—and then stick with it. This is not about trying or needing to be Hollywood skinny. The concept is simply that maintaining a healthy lifestyle yields many benefits for your mind and body—and even your wallet—such as fostering a sense of discipline and structure, looking great in your favorite bathing suit come summertime, or saving the money you would have wasted on too many cocktails! (And, for that matter, if your weight keeps fluctuating all the time, you'll have to keep buying new wardrobes and spending hundreds on fat-versus-skinny jeans!)

Go-Getter Girl Liberty Harper-Simonsen, age twenty-eight, who founded Liberty Fitness gyms in Texas at the age of just twenty-one and became one of the youngest franchisors in the country when it expanded a year later, can attest that exercising and being fit really is about more than looking good in one's favorite pair of Hudsons. As a personal trainer at her ladies-only gyms, she's observed thousands of women experience a complete 180-degree shift in their state of mind before and after just one workout. "I've seen women walk into the gym—actually, drag themselves into the gym—completely down on themselves, saying they feel so awful because, say, they overate the night before and think they ruined their diet," she says. But then—after a little peptalking from Liberty, the quintessential upbeat coach—they'll complete their exercise session and leave the gym saying that they feel good about themselves and have a whole new outlook on the day. "I've even had clients tell me, 'I wasn't going to have coffee with my friend, and now I will!'" Liberty says.

Liberty sees this change of heart as a manifestation of a deeper principle: whether it's politically correct or not to say so, women often associate how we feel about our bodies with how we feel about our lives. You could blame this fact on everything from Foucaultian theories on gender and power to the media-propagated pressure to be thin to one's childhood experiences with food—and certainly there are many fabulous books out there you might consult that would tackle these complex issues. However, from the Go-Getter Girl perspective, the practical reality is that being fit is a big confidence booster! "Who doesn't feel better about themselves when they're eating right and working out?" says Liberty.

In fact, following an exercise regimen can dramatically improve your sense of self in two ways. First, Liberty says, you ironically begin to dissociate your body image with the number on the scale because you start to feel stronger, both physically and mentally. "It's noticing that last week you could only do five push-ups, but this week you can do ten! That's different than simply losing a pound," she says. "Simply knowing you have that *strength* can make you feel powerful, and you'll become more assertive in everyday life—even at work."

Second, it's about the confidence you gain from setting a goal for yourself and achieving it. Says Liberty, "Sticking to a routine can seem so unattainable for people, but if you do it, it fuels you! You think, '*I did it!*' and feel so proud." Liberty has seen that when a client works hard to stick to a routine and meets her goal—whether that's losing ten pounds, eating healthier foods each day, or just making it to the gym four times a week—she not only feels a huge sense of accomplishment but is simply happier and less stressed out. "I've had clients tell me that once they started working out, they stopped snapping at their kids and husbands."

GGG Nugget of Wisdom: *Finding a healthy eating and workout regimen that works for you is not about striving to be a size 2. It's about feeling good about and taking care of yourself so you can fulfill all of your Go-Getter Girl potential!*

Liberty has not only seen that working out changes her clients' spirits; she's experienced such a change herself. At different points in her life, Liberty watched the scale tip too far in both directions—from nearly starving herself after a family move in her teens to being thirty pounds overweight as a

GGG Guide:
To Gym or Not to Gym?

For many budget-conscious young women, joining a gym can seem like a waste of money: why pay a fee to sweat, when you can just run in the park for free? Well, that's fine if you actually do put on your running shoes and hit the pavement. If not, you may need to join a dedicated exercise location. As Liberty's clients found, just showing up at the gym makes it virtually impossible to throw in the towel and give up working out that day. Here are a few key dos and don'ts to help you pick the right spot:

- Do pick a gym that is super clean and has up-to-date equipment. Bonus points for amenities in the locker room, like free razors and nice lotion.

- Do test out the gym before you sign anything. Legit places offer at least one free workout; many offer free two-week memberships or a few trial group-fitness classes. (And if it's not advertised, ask for it anyway.)

- Do ask around to friends, colleagues, and acquaintances about what are the best gyms in the neighborhood. Usually people who have lived in the area for a while know where the gems are and can break down what groups of people go where (e.g., stockbrokers are at gym X, stay-at-home moms are at gym Y).

- Do look for a gym that has adequate facilities for how you like to work out. If you love to swim, make sure there's a great pool. If you love fitness classes, make sure the studio and teachers are up to par.

- Don't break the bank. Your monthly gym membership shouldn't be any more than, say, you would allow yourself to spend on a great date-night top. Depending on your budget, that could be $29 or $150. Also, take advantage of discounts. Many spots offer student or summer memberships for lower fees.

- Don't pick a place that's too far from your house or office, depending on when you tend to work out. If it takes more than fifteen minutes to get there, you know you're not going.

- Don't get suckered. If the salesperson pressures you to buy, look elsewhere.

young adult—before finding her own mind-and-body comfort zone. Though she never received therapy for what would likely be categorized anorexia in her teens, with support from her family, Liberty "snapped out of it" and gained back the weight. In addition, she discovered cardio kickboxing and credits it with helping pull her out of the vicious spiral of negative body image. The classes made her feel empowered, whereas for much of her childhood she was sidelined from sports because of asthma. "With kickboxing, I felt like 'I can be a tough girl, too!'" she says. "That opened the door to the big change."

Liberty studied and became a certified personal trainer at age seventeen and began teaching kickboxing and aerobics classes around her native San Diego. Having found her life's passion, she soon became a co-owner of two Curves franchises with her family, then branched out on her own to form Liberty Fitness. Now that she's sold the company, she's often training for a race or triathlon with her husband to stay in shape, and fitness is part of her life, instead of her life's work. But it's still just as important. "It's a mental-release thing," she says.

Go-Getter Girl Bonnie Fuller would agree. In fact, Bonnie, the former editorial director for *American Media* and editor of *US Weekly*, who is credited with inventing celebrity journalism as we know it during her tenure at the latter, believes that the simple act of working out may have saved her life. "I had two big bouts with depression in my twenties," she told me. "Back then, I remember somebody telling me that exercise would help fight depression, and I found it worked. [Twenty years later] studies have now come out that show exercise really is a depression reliever. So, my workouts are really a 'sanity saver' on multiple levels."

Fuller says that her five-or-six-day-per-week workouts—done in the morning, so she gets it out of the way and the workout doesn't get bumped by some office crisis later on—release stress and give her the energy and endorphins to tackle her long days. "Working out is so good for you—in terms of keeping you healthy, fighting disease, slowing down the aging process. It's beyond vanity to invest time in your life to exercise. It's a healthy thing to do."

Of course, on the vanity side of things, having worked in and around the fashion industry, Fuller does like stylish clothes and cares about her figure—and, as any pragmatic GGG knows, that comes with a price: "I really like to eat," she says, "and if I didn't work out, I wouldn't be able to eat the way I wanted to!"

GGG Nugget of Wisdom: *When it comes to exercise, just do it! Exercise helps release stress, lifts your mood, and minimizes the impact of the wine/chocolate/pizza/margaritas you know you'll want from time to time!*

Now, what if you're thinking, I'm so busy, how can I find the time to work out regularly? Well, in accordance with the Go-Getter Girl philosophy that we'll see throughout this book, you must find a way! Or, as a matter of fact, as Bill Peck said in *The Go-Getter* by Peter B. Kyne, "It shall be done!" For example, GGG Julia Novy-Hidesly, the executive director of the nonprofit Lemelson Foundation in Portland, Oregon, as well as a wife, mom of two kids, and member of many community and professional boards, says that she typically forgoes all social lunches. "During the workday I'm either working or exercising. I eat lunch at my desk." In fact, not one to just pound out the minutes on the Stairmaster, Julia might be seen joining a full-court basketball game on her midday break at the gym, where she can hold her own with the boys; she actually used to play semipro ball for the Portland Saints. In addition, both as a way to be more "green" and to incorporate more fitness into her lifestyle, Julia bikes to and from work, which is a ten-minute downhill jaunt in the morning and a thirty-minute uphill ride in the evening. "I like it because it gives me a moment to unwind and prepare for re-entry to the house," she says. Julia, an avid practitioner of Ashtanga yoga, has, when she's traveled for work in the past, always brought her yoga mat (which was worn so thin it could fit in her briefcase), swim cap, goggles, and running sneakers. Her attitude sums up the Go-Getter Girl perspective on squeezing in workouts: "I don't allow obstacles to get in my way of exercising."

Still need more points of reference? It does take discipline and perseverance, but many well-known Go-Getter Girls have found a way to fit exercise into their lives. Consider the following examples:

- Designer Tory Burch, who manages her successful eponymous clothing business and a household full of kids, still manages to squeeze in daily workouts at 6 A.M.—before she wakes the kids up and takes them to school.

- Ellie Krieger, the host of Food Network's *Healthy Appetite* and former director of nutritional services at the acclaimed La Palestra Center for Preventative Medicine, shared with *Cooking Light* (March 2007) that she does at least twenty minutes of exercise a day—even if she's working eighty hours a week.

- Reporter Lisa Ling—who seems to manage about twelve jobs (!) trotting the globe as a contributor to the *Oprah Winfrey Show*, CNN, *National Geographic Ultimate Explorer*, and *Nightline*—has said to *Runner's World* (August 2004) that she aims for 45 minutes of running, six times a week.

- Supermodel turned Bravo host Niki Taylor, who has said it was hard being a single mom to two boys and find time for fitness, tries to work out three times a week, aiming for 30 minutes of cardio on the elliptical, bike, or treadmill, according to *Fitness* magazine (May 2008). She often mixes in free weights, i.e., doing 10 minutes of cardio, then three sets of weights, then 10 more minutes of cardio, and so on.

- Tony-nominated actress Kelli O'Hara, who most recently starred in *South Pacific* on Broadway (that means at least eight full-length performances a week), runs about three miles, three to four times a week. "Whatever I can do to shake up my body," she says. For Kelli, it's also a much-needed 25 minutes or so of personal time to think through things or memorize songs.

GGG Guide:
Feel the Burn

So you refuse to give up your tall caramel macchiato (*as if!*). Well, that daily trip to Starbucks can clock up to 270 calories. GGGs don't deny themselves, but at the end of the day, it's all about choices. Here's how many calories you could burn during one hour of various activities (based on a 154-pound person). Call it food for thought!

Activity	Approximate Calories Burned per Hour
Walking (3.5 mph)	280
Hiking	370
Running/Jogging (5 mph)	590
Weight lifting (vigorous effort)	440
Cycling (vigorous effort)	590
Dancing	330
Swimming (freestyle laps)	510
Yard Work / Gardening	330
Stretching	180

*Source: Centers for Disease Control and Prevention Web site (adapted from Dietary Guidelines for Americans 2005).

Maybe you're thinking to yourself, okay, but these women all have lots of money and people to help them get in shape, like nutritionists and probably personal trainers. Maybe so, but have you considered that maybe it's worth it for you to invest in some professional help for a period of time? Erika Clarke, a GGG originally from Santa Cruz, California, and a producer at MTV, found that a personal trainer was the answer to her self-admitted workout "bs-ing." "I'm lazy," she admits. "I need structure. By working out with a trainer, I realized I needed a drill sergeant!" Erika used a trainer to help her shed twenty pounds, which not only gave her greater confidence but also instilled a new sense of discipline. "It helped me not to procrastinate— and it gives me something to look forward to besides the monotony of the 'day-to-day,'" Erika says. Plus, because many of her family members have a history of being overweight, she was anxious not to let "feeling a little frumpy after the holidays" progress to more serious concerns down the road. "A lot of people in my family have had health issues," she says. "As I get older, it's important to develop this healthy pattern. So maybe I should be saving more money, but it's for a good cause." In other words, for Erika, the "cost-benefit" of a trainer weighed in favor of the investment. If you are thinking of trying the trainer route, remember that it can be a big emotional and financial commitment. Here are some guidelines for choosing a pro and getting results:

- Make sure that he or she is properly trained and certified.

- Look at the level of fitness and physique of the trainer and his or her clients. It should be one you admire and aspire to. For example, if you're going for lean and lithe, a trainer whose idea of fitness is body-builder bulk is probably not a good match.

- Be wary of trainers that want to lock you in for umpteen sessions. Some form of paying as you go is preferable.

- Look for someone who is a consummate professional. You want to have a good rapport, but your trainer is not really your friend. He or she should be serious enough to kick your butt into shape!

- Trust your gut. If you get a funny vibe or he or she makes you uncomfortable after even the first session, find someone else.

- Ditto for results. If you're not seeing them after a reasonable amount of time (a month or two), assuming you've been keeping up with your diet, move on.

- Don't sleep with your trainer, period!

If you're extra cash conscious, you could even try booking a single session with a trainer to get a program and pointers on form, then go it alone from there. That's what television personality and NBC contributor Maria Menounos did years ago to drop the last twenty pounds of a forty-pound weight loss. "I hired [a trainer] for one [$70] session, and she wrote out for me a general circuit program of jump rope, steps, push-ups, sit-ups, squats, and lunges," Maria shared in *Fitness* magazine in October 2008. "In fact, I still have the piece of paper in case I regain the weight."

While having a trainer can be great, it's certainly not the only way to get motivated for fitness. Go-Getter Girls who are already fitness buffs might rely on cardio or dance classes, videotapes, or simply some new songs on their iPod to get them excited to work out. Some exercise with friends or significant others. Some sign up for 5Ks, minitriathlons, or cycling races to give them something to train for. Others look for a Pilates or yoga instructor whose mind-body-spirit approach really clicks with them. Some who simply can't stand the gym make a point to walk everywhere—always taking the stairs or parking in the farthest spot away in the parking lot or, if they are city gals, shunning cabs and the subway. The key is just finding a method that works for you and making it a true part of your healthy, GGG lifestyle!

GGG Nugget of Wisdom: *It's not always easy to get motivated to work out. Experiment with different types of workouts, sports, and activities to combat boredom and stay enthused. And, yes, sometimes you really will just have to* force *yourself to exercise.*

Get started on your fitness plan by thinking of some definitive objectives. Below, write out three workout goals and come up with three "action steps" to achieve each. Try to think of goals that are feasible and manageable. You don't want to throw in the towel on day one!

FITNESS GOAL #1

Action Steps

1.

2.

3.

FITNESS GOAL #2

Action Steps

1. _____

2. _____

3. _____

FITNESS GOAL #3

Action Steps

1. _____

2. _____

3. _____

Now for the other half of the battle when it comes to maintaining a healthy body: eating right. For this one, Go-Getter Girls will attest that there's simply no quick fix or magic bullet—especially when you've got a schedule jam-packed with a demanding job, work dinners and cocktail parties, dating, socializing with friends, and family events—not to mention traveling and vacations, which can act like quicksand to your healthy eating plan! This book is not a weight-loss or nutrition book—for hardcore diet tips/programs, there are a zillion books out there dealing with those topics. (And we'll review a few of them on page 80, just so you're in the know about popular diet trends!) What this book can offer is the observation that Go-Getter Girls are just as strategic and conscientious when it comes to eating as they are with other areas of their lives. The notion that you'll forever be able to eat and drink whatever you want, all the time, with no consequences to your general health, energy levels, and—let's

GGG Guide:
Exercises on the Go

Before she owned her own nightwear company, GGG Lesley Hatfield was a personal trainer who owned a business called Fitbreaks, which gave midday, mini-exercise classes for employees in large corporations. Lesley says that yes, even if you're stuck in a cubicle all day, or on business travel living in a cramped hotel room, you can stay in shape with easy, effective exercises that don't require more than a few square feet of space. Try the following:

· Push-ups (to tone back and arms and improve posture): Assume a plank position (or modify with knees down) with arms slightly wider than shoulder width. Bend elbows and bend down and push up while holding in your "core." Do two sets of 15 reps.*

· Tricep dips (fights upper-arm jiggle!): Find a sturdy chair or bench. Stand in front of it like you are about to sit, then bend knees and lower hips, placing hands on the seat edge (fingers pointing forward), arms straight. Walk feet out a bit, but keep butt close to chair. With feet flat and chest up, bend and straighten arms. Do two sets of 15 reps.

· Resistance band bicep curls (builds arm strength): Grab an Xertube or Theraband (i.e., those stretchy resistance bands). Hold the band in your hands, wrap it around hands to create resistance, and step on the band with both feet,

*If you hate counting reps, try watching a clock and do as many reps as you can for 30 seconds for each set of the exercises.

so equal lengths of the band are at your sides. Hold forearms slightly lower than perpendicular to body. Curl up to your shoulders, and lower. Do two sets of 15 reps.

- Wall sit-squat (allover leg toner and strengthener): Stand with your back against the wall and with your feet a few feet out in front of you. Squat down with your back and butt flat against the wall until your legs form a 90-degree angle with the ground. Hold for 30 seconds to one minute. Feel the burn! Repeat once.

- Standing lunges (tightens the butt and thighs): Stand erect. Step out with your left foot and lower hips until your left leg forms a 90-degree angle with the floor. Make sure your knee doesn't go past your ankle. Using your glutes, push off your left leg to return to original standing position. Repeat with your right leg. Do two sets of 15 reps, alternating right and left legs.

- Forearm plank (works core and arms): Lie on your belly with legs together. Lift up slightly to place elbows underneath your shoulders and forearms in a triangle position with hands forming a fist. Lift up onto your toes into a plank position, trying to keep your body in one long straight line, with pelvis tipped forward, belly pulled up, and holding your belly button pulled to your spine. Hold plank for 30 seconds to one minute. Repeat once. (Advanced: Do a full, straight arm plank with wrists directly underneath your shoulders.)

- Bicycle crunches (ultimate waist whittler!): Lie on your back, arms behind your head with one hand on top of the other (i.e., not laced). Place legs in

(continued)

face it—physique, is absurd! Go-Getter Girls accept this reality and plan and choose accordingly.

For instance, GGG Lesley Hatfield, a personal trainer-cum-founder of moisture-wicking sleepwear line NiteSweatz who maintains a superfit, trim physique, says that in our "supersize" society, you simply have to think about what you eat—and sometimes that does mean forcing yourself to choose healthy options! Because Lesley's schedule is often filled with eighty-hour workweeks running her business, travel for trade shows and TV appearances, and being a wife and mother, she uses a variety of strategies to "sneak" healthy eating into her day. Each morning she likes to get a nutrient boost with a shot of green veggie juice, and because she often feels too lazy to mix it up, she tells herself that she won't have her morning tea until she downs the shot of liquid veggies. "I make it part of my routine—just like brushing your teeth," she says. In addition, when it comes to managing her calorie count, Lesley says that, no, she doesn't eat whatever she wants—but she also doesn't deprive herself. For example, when we met for breakfast, she ordered some tasty scrambled eggs, hash browns, and iced tea and asked the waitress to hold the toast that usually comes with the meal. Why? "I really wanted some of those hash browns because they looked so good! But the toast would have probably sat there—or I would have eaten something I don't really need," she says. When it comes to eating a well-balanced diet, she tries to eat a mix of fresh, colorful foods to get a variety of vitamins and minerals. If she's making breakfast for her son Jack and notices she's got a yellow plate with just eggs and a banana, she'll make a point to add some more color variety with a bit of veggies. Above all else, Lesley *keeps it simple* when it comes to preparing healthy meals: "Many nights at our house, dinner is a salad made with [pre-washed/boxed] field greens with some protein like grilled chicken or fish on top." For Lesley, such a meal is so easy to prepare that it prevents her from "dodging" eating health-fully with the excuse that she's too exhausted to make dinner. "It's about making the choices to commit to your health—and it relates to your entire life."

As Lesley points out, just like with any other goal in life, Go-Getter Girls know that eating healthy and

GGG PEARL:
On Healthy Snacking

As a Go-Getter Girl, oftentimes your day is a nonstop whirlwind of activity—but you still need to eat! Stalking the vending machine at 4 P.M. can lead to a dietary crash and burn, so here are some ideas for healthy, filling snacks that won't weigh you down (hint: you may have to pack ahead):

- handful of raw nuts, such as cashews, walnuts, or almonds
- 1 cup dry, crunchy bran cereal with some raisins or dried cranberries
- drinkable yogurt, like Dannon Frusion
- sliced apple or banana with a bit of peanut butter
- a hearty nutrition bar from brands like Think, Odwalla, Kashi, or Clif
- 4- or 6-ounce yogurt (try the Greek style!) or cottage cheese, with cinnamon
- low-fat mozzarella string cheese (yes, just like the kind you ate in second grade)

(continued)

(continued from previous page)
- small bowl of oatmeal
- sliced veggies such as carrots, cucumber, or red pepper
- 2 ounces of dried fruit, such as apples, mangoes, or plums
- 1 cup edamame
- 1-ounce package of Flat Earth Baked Veggie Crisps Farmland Cheddar (borderline junk food but cures your jones for something salty/crunchy!)

maintaining your ideal figure does not, for most people, happen by accident! Moreover, eating nutritiously is not just about maintaining your weight—it's about maintaining your energy levels and vibrancy so that you can deal with all the other professional and life obstacles that come your way. Again, the key is finding a plan or routine that works for you. To give you some ideas, here are some general GGG tips to get a healthy-eating jump start:

- Drink lots of water.

- Eat a nutritious, healthy breakfast.

- Stop eating when you are full—really.

- Eat lots of fresh or frozen fruits and vegetables.

- Get enough lean protein: chicken or turkey (no skin); eggs or egg whites; or white, nonoily fish (such as halibut or tilapia).

- Limit consumption of white sugars and carbohydrates (bagels, white rice, white potatoes), and fried or processed foods.

- Limit your intake of alcohol and caffeine. Ditto for diet soda, which many GGGs avoid based on scientific evidence that it may make you hungrier and on unscientific, purely anecdotal evidence that it causes them to bloat.

- Do not beat yourself up if you go overboard one day or at one meal! Just cut back a little the next day or at the next meal. (On that note, if you went really overboard on, say, vacation and your jeans are way tight, cut out snacks for a few days and/or add an extra couple workouts that week. It's easy to halt and reverse a three-pound weight gain; it's a lot harder when it's ballooned to fifteen!)

- Learn to listen to your body. If you are craving a juicy hamburger, eat one. Otherwise, you know you'll eat everything in your cupboards to compensate!

- If you have zero willpower when it comes to peanut butter, Ben & Jerry's, tortilla chips, chocolate, French bread, or whatever, do yourself a big favor and don't keep large quantities in the house!

- Avoid being famished by eating healthy snacks (see GGG Pearl: On Healthy Snacking, for a sample list).

- Practice portion control. No, you don't have to clean your plate at a restaurant, even if it's a business lunch.

- Organic and low-sodium frozen dinners (like Amy's) can be a great portion-controlled, quick meal when you're exhausted from a long day's work. Eat them in moderation.

- Generally avoiding late-night eating and trying not to snack after dinner can help you maintain your weight. Sip herbal tea instead.

- When it's time to indulge, make sure it's something you really want—and that it fulfills your expectations! If you order the chocolate cake and it tastes just so-so, why are you wasting the calories?

In addition, as part of maintaining a healthy GGG lifestyle, try to get seven to eight hours of sleep most nights. Don't be afraid to catch up on weekends or powernap if you've lost z's because of work or socializing one week; you need to recharge! Try not to smoke. Finally, it almost goes without saying that to fully maximize your Go-Getter Girl potential, don't abuse drugs or alcohol; seek treatment or counseling if you feel you're out of control in this (or any other) department. Through eating a healthy diet, taking care of yourself, and exercising, you can take charge of your fitness and give it its rightful position as a key component of your total wellness and success!

GGG Guide:
Diet Books Decoded

If you are in the market for a weight-loss manual, there sure are a lot of books available. Here is a quick guide to some of the most popular plans out there—so that you'll know what your bff means when she says she's "off bad carbs" this week—even if you're not dieting!

Title/Author	Weight-loss modus operandi	Practicability	Readability
The South Beach Diet, by Arthur Agatston, M.D.	Distinguishes between "good carbs" (fruits, veggies, whole grains) and "bad carbs" (white sugar, white flour, baked goods, highly processed carbs).	B— Too restrictive long term but helps break the	B Ample medical info isn't too science-y;

Title/Author	Weight-loss modus operandi	Practicability	Readability
	You get none of the latter—or any fruit or alcohol—for the first 2 weeks ("Phase 1"). In Phase 2, you reintroduce fruit and low-glycemic carbs (e.g., oatmeal, couscous). Theory is that by reducing bad carbs, you lower insulin levels and release weight.	cycle of sugar cravings. Day-by-day meal plans help the "how-to." Minus for pooh-poohing the role of exercise in weight loss.	features interesting background on how the diet became a national phenomenon.
The Zone, by Barry Sears, Ph.D., with Bill Lawren	Basically same as above: excess carbs lead to excess insulin production, which takes you out of the "zone" and leads to fat storage. Ideal fat-burning metabolic state is created by consuming a 40-30-30 ratio of calories from protein, carbs, and fats, respectively. Ratio is broken into "blocks" (i.e., similar to exchanges) of each nutrient based on your calculated daily protein needs.	B− The block system does simplify the calorie math, but the need to "tightly" control "every meal, every snack, every day" in this ratio sets you up for failure.	C+ Dense talk of "eicosanoids" and "glycogen" makes you want to skip to the actual diet, which doesn't appear till chapter 8!
Dr. Atkins' New Diet Revolution, by Robert C. Atkins, M. D.	In short, sugar and refined carbohydrates are evil. This plan is based on consuming animal proteins, vegetables, and fat.	D+ May work in the short term (e.g.,	C Nearly 400 pages of anticarb

(continued)

Title/Author	Weight-loss modus operandi	Practicability	Readability
	Four-phase approach. In the 2-week first phase—"induction"—you get no more than 20 grams of carbs daily, which translates to 3 cups of "loosely packed" salad greens. Even in the lifetime-maintenance phase, you're not supposed to eat bread or sugar and are encouraged to "binge," if need be, on hard-boiled eggs or controlled-carb chocolate bars.	mass water-weight loss), but any diet with tips on dealing with electrolyte-loss leg cramps can't be so healthy—or sustainable.	manifesto, laced with pseudo-science sales pitch.
French Women Don't Get Fat, by Mireille Guiliano	Outlines a 2-day magical-leek-soup fast to jump-start your body "recasting"—a 3-month plan to eliminate your "usual suspects" of dietary offenders. Advocates slow, deliberate, all-senses eating "for pleasure"; "ritual" preparation and eating of meals; eating 50% on your plate for portion control. Champions homemade and all things champagne (Guiliano is the CEO of Veuve Cliquot, by the way).	C+ Useful cross-cultural insights to assess your eating habits, but for serious weight loss, lacks "there-there."	A Vibrant and memoir-y tone, like a sunny stroll down Parisian memory lane.

Title/Author	Weight-loss modus operandi	Practicability	Readability
5-Factor Diet, by Haley Pasternak, M.Sc., with Myatt Murphy	All about multiples of 5: eat 5 times a day, 5 categories of foods each meal (protein, low-glycemic carbs, healthy fats, fiber, sugar-free beverages). Includes Pasternak's famous workout plan, which is 25 total minutes broken into (naturally) 5-minute bursts of exercise. Requires a cheat day each week for "catharsis"!	B+ Tricky, but not impossible, to eat the right combo of foods at the 3-hour intervals recommended.	A- Only about 70 substantive pages; celeb-client quotes add insider-y and inspiring pizzazz.

6

Wardrobe Building 101

*L*et's start from the premise that in this world, looks matter, period. The idea is not that *beauty* matters but that when you present yourself—particularly at work—someone is always taking your measure! This lesson was learned early in life by GGG Nancy Lublin, the former law student who founded Dress for Success, an international organization to help women go from welfare to work by providing suits and career resources to low-income women. When Nancy was growing up, her father, who was a lawyer, once told her that when he needed to hire a new secretary at his office, he would watch the candidate walk from her car to the building and know by the time she walked in the door whether or not he would hire her. What was he observing? How she was dressed and the way she carried herself. "I thought it was horrible, but I realized it was true," Nancy says. "When you see someone walk in the room, you know immediately if you want to date them, hire them, or even be their friend." Nancy believes a first impression can be as much about someone's natural presence as it is about the logistics of looking pulled together and appropriate. She says, "You know when your mom said, 'Don't worry what the other kids think'? She was lying! She also told you not to wear jeans with holes in them—and to comb your hair!"

Her father's story—which, Nancy says, he's not even embarrassed that she tells!—made Nancy particularly cognizant of the importance of appearance at interviews. "Interview clothing is a uniform," she says. "You couldn't walk onto a baseball field without a proper uniform—and it's the same with any other job. It's the first representation of yourself, but it's unfortunate that not everybody has access to the same stuff, and it becomes very classist." To help solve this problem, back when she was just twenty-three and a "miserable" law student, Nancy had an idea to create an organization that would provide proper interview suits and clothing for women trying to get back on their feet. Armed with an unexpected $5,000 inheritance check, advice from a law professor, and help from three nuns in Spanish Harlem, Dress for Success was formed. Over the years, the organization expanded to more than eighty-five locations worldwide and has served more than 400,000 women not only with clothing provisions but also with programs offering employment retention and support—all premised on the notion that what you wear can affect the way you feel and how you're perceived, as well as open or close the doors to opportunities.

Now married with two kids, Nancy has left Dress for Success and is currently CEO of another not-for-profit, Do Something, an organization that promotes volunteerism for teenagers. Even in the Facebook culture of her current workplace, Nancy's concept of the role of one's appearance holds true. "I work in an organization that works with teenagers. If I rocked a pinstripe pantsuit and pearls they'd be like, 'Who's that freaky old lady?' Wearing jeans and Converse sneakers is part of my legitimacy now," she says.

Nancy consciously decides to dress down as part of her credibility these days, but notice one key point: she's the *CEO* of her organization. She's the head boss—the person who doesn't so much have to prove herself but runs the company and sets the tone for office culture. If you're just starting out in your career or working your way up, you are by definition not in Nancy's position! Regardless of what the top players are wearing, how you dress from day to day can affect your advancement at your workplace—and the rate of it.

Take the example of GGG Erika Clarke, whom we met in the previous chapter, and who partially credits her corporate climb at MTV to an ironic fashion choice. Though her path from intern to senior producer involved a lot of hard work, it also involved a pair of jeans—or lack thereof. A very young-looking woman in her midthirties, Erika says that she rarely wears jeans because she wants to convey a mature, professional—but still fashionable—look.

She is "very conscious" of what she wears. "It's easy in [MTV] culture to get really casual, like flip-flops. Sometimes I see these young whippersnappers running around here wearing whatever. But it's still a job. You need to come across that way." For Erika, that translates to always wearing heels, covering up a bit (like pairing a summer dress with a little blazer), and, as mentioned, forgoing most denim. "Especially if it's frayed—I refuse to wear frayed jeans to work!" she says.

MTV was an environment where, if you looked at just clothing alone, the line between bosses and interns was somewhat blurred, with senior managers sometimes dressing in jeans and T-shirts, much like at similarly teen-focused Do Something that Nancy Lublin leads. Erika set herself apart by dressing more professionally, instead of less. "Overall, people at the *top* might dress like they're in college, but people who are *on their way up* dress more conservatively," she says. Erika built a reputation as a sharp professional by dressing the part, and it paid off. She worked her way up from intern to producer in nine years, as those around her dropped like flies in the competitive environment.

Now, you may be thinking that this is too superficial—that your credentials and accomplishments should speak for themselves and that you should be promoted solely on merit and not on your appearance. Well, the fact of the matter is that in many careers, those two spheres, appearance and opportunities, overlap. The way you dress—if you look polished and professional—can make your superiors take notice and think you must be organized and on the ball. Conversely, if you look disheveled and messy all the time, it can hold you back. Politics whiz Jen Bluestein, from chapter 4, says she's noticed when interns arrived in casual tank tops or shorts every day—and her impression was not good. "When they looked sloppy, it said to me: you are not paying attention, because *I'm* not dressed like that—and [the other full-time employees] in the office aren't dressed like that!" The more unfortunate impression it gave her (perhaps inadvertently) was that the young women didn't want to advance. Jen puts it bluntly: "When you work in a role that's external—that is, a role in which you come in contact with the press or the public or clients or even senior management—in general, you will never get promoted if you look like crap! You won't be given more responsibility."

With that big picture in mind, let's get down to some basic strategies for choosing professional attire. First, there's the interview. Here are some key dos and don'ts:

- Do err on the side of conservative.

- Even if it's a creative profession (e.g., marketing, media, design), do not wear a sleeveless top or tank top to an interview. If it's hot, commute sleeveless and slip on your blazer before you arrive.

- If appropriate for the industry, do consider wearing a well-fitting, tailored dress (knee length).

- For traditional professions such as law, banking, politics, or accounting, wear a suit in a dark, neutral color (navy, black, gray). It may sound chauvinist, but consider wearing a skirt suit as opposed to pants. This isn't about showing leg; rather, your interviewers may consider skirts the more "formal" choice for a woman.

- If you're in a skirt, do wear sheer nude stockings—even if it's summertime. It simply looks more pulled together and professional. In the movie *Disclosure*, Demi Moore plays a boss who sexually harasses her male employee. Demi's character usually appears to be wearing a skirt suit with no stockings. What's the message being sent here?! Also, don't wear black stockings. Black *tights* are a different story and totally permissible in winter (and, side note, the black Terrific Tights by Assets are particularly fabulous!). But as GGG editor Bonnie Fuller has said, an interviewee in sheer black stockings may scream "escort service!"

- Do not wear open-toed shoes or flip-flops.

- Do wear good-condition heels and carry a simple, worky bag with some structure to it.

- When in doubt, do tuck in your shirt.

It's great to be fashionable, but once you've gotten your stiletto-clad foot in the door, think of this default rule when you select your work outfits each day: go for neat and conservative over trendy and sloppy. To further explain, check out the matrix on page 90 for a Go-Getter Girl point of view on wardrobe styles.

First, you *always* want to be somewhere in the upper hemisphere labeled as "neat." As a default, your work clothes should be clean and well pressed, with simple lines and a bit of structure. Even being in the "boring" quadrant (think light pink twinset and gray slacks) is infinitely better than being sloppy. As a general rule, the sweet spot of work dressing is probably in the upper right quadrant: a *stylish* but not too trendy, decidedly neat and tidy ensemble. On the fashion scale, as GGG Isabel González puts it, "You want

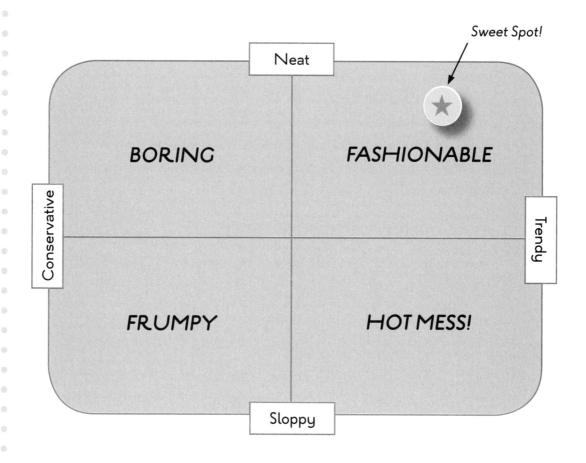

Sweet Spot!

Neat

Conservative

Trendy

BORING

FASHIONABLE

FRUMPY

HOT MESS!

Sloppy

to make a statement—but you can make a statement at 80 percent, rather than 150 percent." Why? First, you're demonstrating a certain amount of creativity and flair—without seeming like a slave to fashion who is more concentrated on her outfits than business. Second, it's supremely difficult (and not necessarily advisable in all professions) to pull off a 100 percent neat *and* trendy work ensemble. I'm talking about the kind of outfits you see in the fashion spreads of *Lucky* magazine, where somehow the model looks perfect—and perfectly work appropriate—with her ivory tulip skirt, yellow-print diaphanous blouse, camel-colored ankle boots, lavender minijacket, and ginormous amethyst pendant that "pulls it all together"! Unless you're a total pro at self-styling, you will likely end up in something that misses the mark in terms of proportion or sizing and drops you down to the "sloppy" (aka "hot mess") category. Of course, if you actually work in fashion, design, or art, you'll get more leeway into the trendy category—but, bottom line, you never want your clothing choices to undermine your professionalism.

○ **GGG Nugget of Wisdom:** *You know the saying "Dress for the job you want, not the job you have"? Believe it.*

Remember: to a great extent, the style image you present can also help funnel you toward opportunities or career paths because people will cast you in a certain role based on your appearance. For example, if, as mentioned earlier, you are gunning for a job as a fashion editor, then it will help to display some of that of-the-moment fashion sense and imagination in your outfits on a daily basis. Or, if your goal is to become a manager at a brokerage firm, you would want to choose impeccably tailored suits, with maybe a pop of a "power" color in your blouse. Also, take a look around—what does your dream-job boss wear? Does he or she wear tailored slacks even though the employees technically can wear jeans on Fridays? When it comes to fashion, follow the lead of the professionals in your space whom you aspire to be like. Your clothing selections contribute to your overall image, and a GGG's image is sparkling, crisp, and always professional!

To help you get started, the first professional attire tip to have in mind is to *keep it simple.* Many stylish GGGs I interviewed compared their daily business-casual wardrobes to an adult form of "Garanimals" (the mix-and-match outfits for kids!): blouse, neutral pair of trousers or skirt, and a nice pair of heels (under their desk!)—with flip-flops or comfy slip-ons in their bag for commuting. Or, if they travel for work, their go-to look is a jersey-type dress that easily rolls up to stuff into their carry-on. Simplify the shopping process even more by figuring out a handful of brands that work for you almost every time—to the point where you can guess the size you would wear of any given garment by that designer. Then, you can embrace online shopping, which can be an invaluable option when your schedule is too packed to spend even thirty minutes at the mall!

The next big tip is to make sure you *shop for mainly career-clothing lines,* unless you're in an ubercreative field that requires a more eclectic look. A common, inadvertent mistake a get-along girl might make is wearing clothing that is cut and geared for socializing instead of for work (e.g., sorority-girl tight black pants from Guess). Even if you want to be stylish, you need a threshold number of actual "career"-category clothing so that you don't look like an intern playing dress-up for work! For reasonably priced pieces, Ann Taylor and Ann Taylor Loft are the go-to spots. Also try Banana Republic, J. Crew, Club Monaco, Zara, Nine West (for shoes—they've gotten much more stylish lately), or Loehmann's and Marshalls (for great deals on, say, Tahari or Michael Kors pieces). Among department stores, Lord and Taylor is known for its great career clothes and sales. If money is less of an issue, the worky pieces from lines such as BCBG, Theory, Chaiken, Trina Turk, Nanette Lepore, Diane von Furstenberg, Tory Burch, and Cynthia Steffe—to name just a few—offer a great balance of fashion and professionalism.

GGG PEARL:

On Suiting

Even if you don't work in a corporate environment per se, you need to own a couple of suits. Buying matching suit pieces is a good way to jump-start your GGG wardrobe because you can mix them up: wear the pants on their own regularly, wear the jacket with another skirt or jeans, or wear the top and bottom together when you have an interview or important meeting. Here are some tips for finding your perfect match:

- Your first purchase should be a basic black suit, then buy a couple more neutrals, such as navy, charcoal, or dark brown.

- Unless you already have a big wardrobe of suits or are, say, a TV news-caster, avoid buying brightly colored suits. Even though a pink suit may be a great fashion statement à la Elle Woods, you probably won't get much mileage out of it because everyone will know you wore it last Tuesday. If you are still building your collection, add a stylish and interesting but less-conspicuous suit into your mix by choosing a neutral tweed or pinstripe.

- Look for suits at department stores such as Lord and Taylor, Nordstrom, or Bloomingdale's. In addition, try discount emporiums like Loehmann's, Filene's Basement, or TJ Maxx. Often, these stores have the exact same items you see full price at the mall (aka "overstock").

(continued)

- Expect to pay at least $200.

- Look for first-rate fabrics, such as lightweight wool or *high-quality* synthetic blends; many great designers work with polyester, rayon, viscose, or nylon nowadays. A little bit of stretch (i.e., Spandex or Lycra) is good as well. Avoid linen or khaki suits; they are a wrinkle nightmare. Also, look for quality construction: straight, matching seams; sewn-in instead of glued linings; well-sewn buttons.

- Do you go lined or unlined? Jackets and skirts should be lined, but for pants, it's a personal preference. Many of the more stylish makers, such as Theory or BCBG, nix the pant lining on lighter weight fabrics for a more modern look and feel.

- Here are some markers of a good fit: In the jacket, shoulder seams should be centered on the top of your shoulders. You should have enough room in the upper arms and back to allow full range of motion (i.e., hold your arms out to the side), while still creating a fitted shape. When your arms hang straight down, the sleeve cuff should fall between the wrist bone and top of your hand. You should be able to fit two fingers in the waistband comfortably. Pants should smoothly drape down your backside, not cling or hug, especially not to the bottom half of your tush. Skirt lengths should be at or just above the knee. Pencil skirts should not ride up. In short, buy something looser off the rack and bring it to your trusted tailor.

- Keep in mind what you will be wearing underneath. You'll usually wear a button-down or knit top beneath your jacket (i.e., no flimsy camisoles!), so make sure there's enough room to accommodate. Or you may be looking at one of those new-style jackets that button all the way up the front and are worn more like a shirt. Even then, make sure there is room for a lightweight undershirt to absorb sweat. Hint: Try an uberthin, moisture-wicking T-shirt from brands like Autrepeau or Uniqlo.

In addition, think about this key GGG concept for wardrobe building: cost versus cost per wear. It's the relation between the cost of an item of clothing compared with the number of times you will wear it. Take, for example, a pair of perfect light-wool black pants priced at $200. Let's assume that you're going to be wearing them a couple times a week for a whole year—the cost per wear is less than $1! Conversely, say you're considering a blue sequined dress that's perfect for your New Year's date—but you'll never wear again—for the same price. That's, well, $200 per wear. What's the better investment?

Think about the pieces in your wardrobe that will be your signature staple pieces. One GGG businesswoman told me about a black Victorian-styled Tracy Reese suit jacket she bought years ago: it cost maybe $350, but she feels great whenever she wears it to an important meeting. "I was very strategic about this piece!" she says. "I couldn't commit the resources to my wardrobe that other people maybe could—but with this piece, it stands out and makes an impact. I get compliments on it every time! That's how I know it was a good buy." As you allocate your wardrobe budget, you want to have staple pieces you invest in, buying the best-quality, best-fitting items you can within the parameters of your budget. These would include the following:

GGG CHECKLIST:

Twenty-One Pieces of Office Attire Every GGG Needs in Her Closet:

- ☐ 2 pantsuits
- ☐ 1 skirt suit
- ☐ black dress pants
- ☐ white stretch button-down (tailored)
- ☐ pointy-toed black pumps
- ☐ 1 wrap dress or shirt dress
- ☐ black pencil or trumpet skirt
- ☐ black opaque tights
- ☐ black or navy cocktail dress
- ☐ 2 stylish twinsets
- ☐ chunky pearls
- ☐ simple stud or small hoop earrings
- ☐ dark, tailored "work" jeans
- ☐ 3 well-fitted T-shirt bras (two nude, one black)
- ☐ Burberry-like trench coat, in a neutral color such as khaki or army green
- ☐ control undergarment, like Spanx Power Panties or nude control-top stockings
- ☐ structured handbag

- jeans
- black dress pants
- two suits
- white button-down shirt(s)
- bras
- winter coat
- work pumps
- handbag

Other wardrobe items, however, can be purchased on the cheap—such as trendy going-out tops or dresses (you know you'll want something new each time you have a hot date!) or accessories like earrings, belts, and bracelets. Your personal style will also determine if you put things like T-shirts and tank tops (can they ever survive more than a season?), summer frocks, trendy jackets, or leggings in your cheapie category. The favorite GGG cheapie spots? Forever 21 by a landslide, followed by H&M and Target (for accessories). Falling in the midrange of your wardrobe budget allocation will likely be your work-style blouses, knit sweaters, and seasonal skirts, which may cost more than your "budget" purchases because these need to be made well enough to survive regular wear and dry cleaning. (Although sometimes, even these can be bargain purchases if you're willing to search a little at the discount spots!)

Whether it's a budget or investment purchase, how do you know when something is quality? GGG designer Julie Chaiken, whose eponymous line of clothing was perhaps the first work-geared bridge clothing line when she launched it in 1994, says that you want to look at the weight and quality of the fabric, refined structural details like good seaming or darting, and, most important, the way it fits your body. As Julie says, "The item should not fit you like a sack!"

Wearing clothes that fit you properly is a key GGG concept, so to expand on this idea a little more, consider the story of GGG Shoshanna Lonstein Gruss, whose popular clothing line was born from her own search for the perfect fit. Always a petite, slim yet curvy girl, Shoshanna could never find clothing that fit her bust and waist at the same time—much less appropriately, without being too sexy. Dresses and halters she found never had enough support or worked with a bra, and bathing suits were the worst; one summer she and some of her girlfriends drove out to a specialty Long Island shop to have bikinis made. "It was our only option—unless we wanted a two-piece that had a skirt to midthigh!" she jokes.

After graduating from college, Shoshanna returned to New York and interviewed for investment-analyst jobs but was still obsessed with the lack of clothing for women who were different shapes and sizes. She sketched out her ideas in a notebook, talked to some family friends in the business, and got an internship at a small lingerie factory, where she basically hung out all day and learned about everything from patterns to muslin to fabric to trade shows. Finally, her dad, a successful businessman, gave her some seed money for a small sample line that she presented in a multiline showroom. A rep from Bloomingdale's had stopped in to see another designer's line but noticed

GGG Guide:
"Support" Systems

One thing every Go-Getter Girl absolutely needs is a good "support" system. Susan Nethero, owner of the Intimacy boutiques in Atlanta, New York, and other major cities, is the goddess of all things bra. Starting from the premise that tape measures don't work when calculating band size, she uses a "holistic and proprietary" method that basically involves eyeing the width of your back and ribs and the shape and slope of your bustline to determine size. For those who may not be able to personally experience the method—or missed Nethero's extensive coverage on *Oprah* in the past few years—here are the life-changing tips I learned from her:

- The most common mistake women make in bra fitting is buying a bra too large in the band size. "Bigger" does not mean more comfort! It actually creates discomfort because the breasts are not properly supported.

- Only 10 percent of a bra's support should come from the straps. The rest should come from the band. That is, you should be able to lower the straps and jump up and down without your breasts moving in the cups. Really. That means a properly fitted bra will initially feel much, much tighter across your bodice than you're used to.

- In an ideally fitting bra, the strap in the back should be EVEN with the bottom of the cups in the front. Think about how a bustier looks—that's the correct alignment, not the image I'm sure you can picture of a woman with the back of the bra rigged all the way up to her shoulder blades trying to "harness" her breasts!

- Bras can be tailored. Tailoring involves simply cutting off the seam where the hook attaches in the back, removing an inch or two in the band, and reattaching the hook plate.

- Fit your bra on the last hook (not the middle one, as commonly thought), so that you can move inward to tighten as the bra stretches out, which it will.

- You really only need three bras: one to wash, one to wear, and one in the drawer. Buy two nudes and one black bra at a time.

Shoshanna's classic shift dresses. "They ended up placing a $30,000 order for our dresses! And that was the beginning," she says. In 2001, she launched her swim collection, which became a huge success as the first line to offer mix-and-match sizing for two-pieces.

Shoshanna's philosophy on fit should be a GGG credo: clothing should be "celebratory" of the body—working with and enhancing your figure without over- or underexposing it. You want to look elegant and appropriate at all times. A dress, for example, should skim your body and shape, but not be too tight around the hips. "There's a fine line between 'fitted' and not being able to walk!" she says. How can you "celebrate" your shape when it comes to clothes? Consider these tips for getting the perfect fit:

Embrace alterations. There's a reason why most women have multiple fittings for their wedding gowns: one simple nip or tuck can make all the difference in the world. When it comes to your everyday wardrobe, a good tailor can turn a reasonably priced purchase into virtual

GGG PEARL:
On Being Prepared

Trust me, there will come a day in your glamorous Go-Getter Girl life when, say, a button pops off of your favorite silk blouse—minutes before you have an important client meeting. At that point, nothing can save you but the strip of double-sided tape from your Go-Getter Girl Office Emergency Kit! Here are the items you should have tucked away somewhere in (or under) your desk:

- pack of double-sided tape
- breath mints or gum
- nail file
- Band-Aids
- wrap sweater (for days when the air-conditioning is blasting)
- backup makeup kit with mascara, powder, and lip gloss
- curling iron
- ponytail holder
- black stilettos

couture! Say you bought a pair of Banana Republic pants on sale that fit your hips but not your slim waist. A tailor can cinch the waist and add some darting for just a few bucks. Tailors can do other amazing things such as remove the pocket linings and sew the pockets shut on your favorite white pants (*ah*, that's how to prevent the X-ray effect!) or sew bra cups into a strapless gown. Sho-shanna once even added some gold beads to the back of a dress to cover a bra strap.

Hem your pants to the right length. The average woman is five feet four—yet most pants nowadays seem cut for a leggy five-feet-ten model. There are some decent options out there for off-the-rack, shorter-length pants (e.g., Joe's Provacateur Jeans or J. Crew petites), but at one point or another you'll have to have a pair of pants hemmed. The rule of thumb: wear the shoes you plan to wear them with and have pants hemmed to between a quarter to a half inch above the floor. For jeans, visit a tailor who knows how to reattach the original hem, and, if you find a ridiculously well-fitting, "holy grail" pair of jeans, consider buying two pairs: one to hem for heels, and one for flats.

- ibuprofen
- tampons
- mini sewing kit (with safety pins)
- toothbrush/toothpaste
- purse-size umbrella
- extra pair of pantyhose and undies for surprise mishaps

Banish ill-fitting button-downs. Curvy women know all too well the egregious emblems of a button-down blouse that doesn't properly fit. First, the shirt should fit easily across your back without any pulling. This means that if you hold your arms out straight in front of you and cross them, the shirt should not feel or look like it will split down the middle of your back! Next, there are those annoying peekaboo spaces between the buttons. As one stylist says, when the spaces between shirt buttons gap, it can make you look like a stuffed sausage, even if you're skinny. Shoshanna suggests choosing button-downs that have some stretch in the fabric or darting around the bust. Also, make sure you are wearing a properly fitted bra (see GGG Guide: "Support" Systems). If that doesn't work, stick a little piece of double-sided tape in the space between the buttons. If the fabric still seems like it's holding together for dear life, buy a size bigger and have shirts tailored or have shirts custom made.

In addition, here are a few special tips for finding perfectly fitting jeans: denim does stretch, so you want to buy the snuggest size you can, so long as

GGG PEARL:
On Laundering Clothes

You don't have to be a domestic goddess to know a few simple tricks for keeping your wardrobe in great shape. Here are some top tips for cleaning your clothes:

· If the label on a garment says "dry-clean only," do so! If it says merely "dry clean" (or for fabrics such as rayon, silk, or cashmere), you can probably hand wash the item in cold water with a gentle detergent.

· Remove your freshly-dry-cleaned items from the plastic when you get home. Your clothing needs to breathe—and the plastic will cause fabrics to yellow.

· In a pinch, mild shampoo can be great for rinsing out delicates while traveling.

· Turn dark jeans inside out before washing to keep them from fading.

· For minor to moderate stains, have an arsenal of tools around the house such

it does not cause muffin top; thong sightings; creases along the front rise of the jeans; creases underneath the butt area, at the top of the thigh; or camel toe. Some experts suggest squatting down in the dressing room for a minute or so to test how much the jeans will stretch. In terms of style, according to GGG Stacy London of TLC's *What Not to Wear*, boot-cut is not necessarily flattering to everyone; it works best on women who are five feet four or taller and have long legs. On shorter women, a boot-cut jean may make the thighs look heavy if the jeans hug too tightly at the knee before they flair out at the leg. Thus, women under five feet four should try straight-leg jeans to elongate the legs. It almost goes without saying that despite trends, skinny jeans are the hardest look to rock; they're best for tall, thin, leggy types. As for the derrière, smaller pockets (4–6 inches) and flap pockets are more flattering on petite women, whereas slightly wider (but unembellished) pockets add nice shape to curvier women's backsides.

Now that you've got your basic GGG wardrobe and fit covered, here's one final point on accessories: ever since *Sex and the City* brought the word *Manolo* into the modern gal's lexicon, the appeal

as Tide or Clorox stain pens, Spray and Wash Dual Power (all-around great stain lifter), Oxyclean stain wipes (handles even lipstick and spaghetti sauce), and Madame Paulette's Professional Stain Removal Kit (known to stave off wedding-dress disasters).

and seeming importance of premier designer shoes and handbags has skyrocketed—but how much is too much to spend? Carrie Bradshaw aside, no Go-Getter Girl really need spend a month's rent on a pair of Jimmys or a Marc Jacobs bag! Even in the recent *Sex and the City* movie, Carrie's label-lusting assistant Louise made do with rentals through Bag, Borrow, or Steal (Netflix for handbags)—until her flush boss bought her a Louis Vuitton for Christmas. This is not a financial-planning book, but I can say that even if you think having a status bag or shoes will open doors, if you really can't afford it, part of you will likely regret the purchase—if not now, five years from now, when you're wondering where the heck all your money for a potential mortgage down payment went! Go-Getter Girls love nice stuff, but they also know the pleasure you get from a new Prada or Gucci (that puts you in debt) will surely be fleeting. To curb buyer's remorse, here are some good rules of thumb to think about when you contemplate a pricey designer purchase. First, there's the love it–leave it method (which, notably, may not be valid for sample sales or other time-sensitive purchases): go home and come back to the store the next day or week. If the item is still there, and you still love it, need it, have to have it, proceed to phase 2. Now, consider: a) Would you even *like* it if it didn't have a swanky designer name on the tag? and b) Can you pay for it in cash—in other words, not on a credit card—without cutting into your rent, mortgage, car, or student-loan payment; 401K contribution; or other life necessity? If not, then put it back and step away from the accessories rack!

Sure, the seventeenth-century English clergyman and historian Thomas Fuller may have said "Good clothes open all doors," but if this phrase were posted in every GGG's closet, it would have a little asterisk and a note saying, "i.e., good clothes that you can afford—even if barely"! And one last reminder: presence isn't just about good clothes—it's about the poise and confidence you exude when you know you are looking and feeling great. So don't slouch, pull your shoulders back and head up, walk with a purpose, and smile! You too will have the effortless, stylish, sophisticated look of a true Go-Getter Girl.

7.

Dress for the Occasion, and Look Fabulous When Fabulousness *Counts*!

GG Robin Meade, star anchor of *Morning Express* on HLN, needs to pay attention to what she wears on a day-to-day basis because, well, millions of people see her on television—*and* critique her style choices. Through competing in beauty pageants and years of broadcasting work, she's learned her own personal rules for how to look fab on air: "I stick to V-necks and jewel tones, rarely turtlenecks," she shared with me a few years ago, "because I can't stand to have things on my neck." For her on-air wardrobe, she invests in expensive pieces by brands like St. John and in designer shoes (even if she rounds out her self-described "boutique meets cheap" outfits with cheapie tank tops and $5 necklaces).

But when she's not working—just hanging out, running errands around town, or meeting up with friends—it's an entirely different clothing story.

Ms. Meade certainly does not pull out all the stops and dress as if she's about to be on camera. Instead, her "off-duty" uniform often includes cheap little sundresses with built-in bras bought for about $14 each at local big-box stores, like Target and Wal-Mart. In the fall, she might wear workout pants and tanks with built-in bras, with maybe a little sweater thrown over the top. Her on-air outfits and her day-to-day outfits are worlds apart. "On air, I have to have a look that means business. Off the air my clothing is more casual, girly, and a little sexy," she has said.

Meade's two different style "worlds"—off and on the air—actually exist for *every* woman, and especially for Go-Getter Girls. In short, there are times when you need to look "on" and totally polished, and there are times when you don't. In the previous chapter, we spoke about the basic importance of building a wardrobe. In this chapter, the focus is distinguishing between dressing for important occasions and dressing for everyday life. For example, if you're going to be on TV like Robin Meade or have an important job interview or social function coming up, you need to think more about and plan out what you wear. But GGGs don't always waste their style energy and money putting together an ideal outfit every time they leave the house. This is a critical distinction because many young women get overwhelmed by the idea that they have to look perfect all the time—or they become intimidated by the old-fashioned idea that you should *always* look your best because you never know whom you might run into. How stressful! Instead, Go-Getter Girls are strategic about outfits, maintaining a nonstressful base level of concern about their clothes or appearance but *really* pulling out the stops if there's a particular moment when a style decision could have a great impact on their professional or social life.

Think about an event to which all girls can relate: a first date with someone you *really* like. You probably spend the whole week (or more!) shopping for and planning what you are going to wear. There are discussions and consultations with girlfriends, mothers, sisters, your guy friend, and your hairdresser about the perfect ensemble. You're thinking about whether you want to come across as sweet or sexy or tomboy chic. If you're not sure it's a *date-date* (e.g., he asks you to meet at the coffee shop to "study"), there's an entirely separate analysis of what jeans and what boots to wear—and how much skin to show (tank top or V-neck tee?)—so that just in case it's not a *date*-date, you won't feel silly.

It's that intense, anxiety-producing yet amazingly exciting phase of a new and promising relationship, which my girlfriends and I often call high-impact dating. We're referring to those key first few dates with a dream man, where you've been thinking about the date nonstop and every outfit is planned out (and probably brand-new) and where you get your most primped before each meeting so that his very first sight of you when he picks you up is an unforgettable image of your most beautiful self, which will hopefully be imprinted in his mind—with indelible ink—forever. Sound stressful? Absolutely! But that's also part of the fun, isn't it? Of course, it's not like you'll keep up the ubercoifed appearance forever. Once the relationship settles in and gets a little more comfy, you'll hang out with him in your carefully orchestrated cute-casual outfits (and ponytail), and then finally—perhaps weeks or months

GGG CHECKLIST:

Nine Key GGG Items for Dressing Up:

- ☐ Spanx Power Panties (or, for more coverage, Spanx Higher Power), or Donna Karan Body Perfect Slimmer
- ☐ strapless bra (nude)
- ☐ nonfaded, "going-out" jeans
- ☐ metallic strappy sandals (in gold or silver)
- ☐ small "going out" purse in black, gold, or silver
- ☐ cake eyeliner
- ☐ lip gloss
- ☐ oil-blotting papers
- ☐ double-sided tape (e.g., Hollywood Fashion Tape or Fashion Fix tape)

in—you will be happy to whip out your favorite ratty T-shirt you've had since junior high. If you'd showed up in that on your first date, would he have been as smitten? Who knows? But it's probably something you never would have tried because you were so intent on making a breath-taking first impression!

Not all that unlike a hot-first-date situation, there will be times in your Go-Getter Girl life where it really *counts* to look good—and it's basic common sense that you'll want to think more about your appearance in these personal "high-impact" moments. Your moment could be simply a meeting with your boss to ask for a raise, a presentation at a conference in front of industry power players, a public or television appearance, or even a hip Fourth of July party—all situations where your strategic sartorial flair will be noticed! Think about A-list actresses—and how memorable style moments helped catapult them to stardom and style-icon status. For example, recall Nicole Kidman in that chartreuse, mandarin-collar John Galliano number at the Oscars in 1997—which fashion site Glam.com called "the dress that started it all." Remember also Halle Berry in her peekaboo, embroidered maroon Elie

Saab dress at the Oscars in 2000. And J.Lo's brilliantly controversial Versace tropical-print scarf dress with carefully placed double-sided tape at the 2001 Grammys.

Why did those looks matter? Because nowadays, a celeb's awards-show dress choice is inherently a high-impact style moment: the image will run through a virtual traveling circus of media coverage! There's the "LIVE! FROM THE RED CARPET!" coverage, followed by the awards show itself, then the postshow commentary (complete with snarky expert analysis of the evening's best and worst ensembles), then the endless layouts in the celeb weeklies, and finally the monthly magazine roundups. No wonder celebrity fashion stylists can charge thousands to select an outfit—in addition to the cost of the clothes! However often a best-dressed actress says she wore "the first thing she tried on" at a design house, there's no way she neglected to at least think about the ensemble she (or her stylist) chose in some strategic way—in terms of how it fit, the color, the fashion forwardness of it—or about whether another actress has worn the dress before. Sure, the entertainment world can be overly superficial, but if you're in the public eye in any capacity, conscientiousness about clothes is important. A good (or bad) style choice will be seen live by millions of people, and the print image can remain in the public consciousness for weeks if not years!

Even if your average work or social event is not *quite* as high profile as a Hollywood awards show (just yet), you too must learn to identify your own personal "public-eye" moments. Go-Getter Girls know how to capitalize when it counts by strategically planning their great outfits based on the level of visibility, fellow company, and potential opportunities at any given event. In short, Go-Getter Girls know how to look fabulous when fabulousness really *counts*!

For example, GGG Kylie Simmons,* age thirty-six and a sales executive from New Orleans, pulls out all the stops whenever she has a big, swanky party to attend. She looks sharp on a day-to-day basis, but a *big* event calls for the "theatrical," she says. On these occasions, she enlists the help of a top stylist to create "theme" ensembles. "My favorite outfit was when we did an Asian theme—from the silk kimono all the way to chopsticks in my hair." Think that was a memorable, show-stopping outfit? You bet, and it is this kind of extra—strategically selected—effort that has earned Kylie a reputation as a fantastic dresser (she was even named a best-dressed woman by a regional magazine).

And gorgeous sisters and GGGs Sophie LaMontagne and Katherine Kallinis, who own the chic Georgetown Cupcake bakery in D.C., trade in their aprons for Manolos when a key style moment presents itself. "Normally, when we're in the shop baking or running errands for the business, we'll wear something comfy, like lululemon pants or Juicy sweats," Katherine says. If they're selling at the counter, they do try to dress up a bit, but nothing super fancy. However, for events such as a recent after-party for the tony White House Correspondents' Association Dinner—which would be flooded with D.C.'s movers and shakers—they turn their fashion meter into high gear! Katherine and Sophie "love to dress up," of course, so for that event they went shopping and bought new dresses, shoes, and accessories and had gone to the spa and gotten their hair blown out and nails done. "I think people were surprised when they saw us!" Katherine jokes. It may seem like a lot of fuss for a party, but going back to a principle from the previous chapter, looking extra great gives you an added self-esteem boost. Says Katherine, "God bless you if you're not afraid to go out to an event and meet people, even [when] you have a bad hair day. I wish I could be like that! It gives me more confidence if I dress well—and we take care of ourselves because it's important." And, as a former event planner for Gucci, she knows that dressing up for a high-profile event can be good for business: "It's about presenting a certain image," she says.

One more point: if you think these busy ladies—who, at the time, rose at the crack of dawn to start baking cupcakes—had all day to shop for their fabulous outfits, think again! Katherine jokes that now she understands why people have personal shoppers, and Sophie reminisces that before they were business owners, they used to spend hours just walking around looking at makeup. "But for this party, we were actually really stressed because we had a small sliver of time to shop on a Monday afternoon between a meeting with our lawyer and another meeting and had to get shoes, a dress, *and* makeup!" Sophie recalls. How did they deal? Says Katherine, "I went to Gucci and tried on a dress and wasn't set on it yet—but after we looked in a couple more places, it came down to a realization that I just cannot go to another store! I had no time to go back to Gucci, so I just had to buy it over the phone." Adds Sophie, "I saw a dress I liked, and they didn't have my size—but they had one in Texas, so I ordered it in my size, hoped it would fit when it came in the mail—and it did!"

In an ideal world, you'd have the luxury to shop and prep for hours for a special event, but the Go-Getter Girl reality is that sometimes you won't. That does not mean you abandon all effort to look extra special! You just have to figure out your tricks to look fabulous in a hurry—whether that means knowing your one-stop-shopping spot to pick up a dress *and* shoes, borrowing a glamorous top and earrings from your fashionista friend, or grabbing a black cocktail dress from your closet and using your one free hour for a professional blow-dry. Broadway actress Kelli O'Hara, for example, laughs about the quick-change strategies she and her live-theater peers use to get "glam" for the Tony Awards. Kelli says, "It's so funny, sometimes I read about [Hollywood actors'] Oscar preparations. They have seventeen different appointments—including one to, say, get their bikini line waxed in the shape of a heart!" On Kelli's big awards-show day, including when she was nominated for her lead role in *South Pacific*, she was at Radio City Music Hall by 8:30 in the morning to rehearse that night's Tony performance in full costume and makeup—then she went back to her own theater to perform a matinée of her show! When the matinée was over, she had exactly thirty-three minutes to take off her wig and costume and have her hair blown dry. Of that moment, she recalls, "I end up with some combo of stage makeup and other makeup and jump in a car to be there to walk the red carpet at 7 P.M. There are no long spa days to prepare—but I do the best I can to look my best for red carpet—even if I end up with a little eyelash glue on my nose!"

GGG Nugget of Wisdom: *Stress, but don't overstress, about creating a look for an important event. If your schedule is packed that week, try online shopping. A few strategic items (a colorful cocktail dress, metallic heels, fantastic earrings, lip gloss) can have a big impact.*

Also, remember that even when the occasion calls, you don't have to spend a million bucks to *look* like a million bucks! Consider this story from GGG Gracia Walker—whose own impromptu high-impact outfit was an unexpected success story of the Sharon-Stone-Gap-T-shirt-at-the-Oscars variety. Before recently taking the leap to launch the personal catering busi-

GGG Guide:
Dress Codes Decoded

In addition to knowing when to strategically pull out all her stylish stops, a GGG also knows the basics of what types of outfits are appropriate for what types of occasions. Check out the chart below for some guidance on often-perplexing dressing etiquette.

Dress Code	Description / Appropriate Attire
Traditional Business	Ladies wear skirt suits or pantsuits, blouses, hosiery, close-toed heels. Men are in suits and ties. Some experts further distinguish a "business formal" category, which requires, for example, that women wear skirted suits and that men wear only French-cuff-style shirts with their suits.
Business Casual	Women can wear pressed dress pants, trousers, crisp khakis, skirts, collared shirts, and knit sweaters (no tanks). For men it's pressed dress pants, trousers, khakis, and collared shirts. No jeans, T-shirts, or flip-flops.
Cocktail Attire, Semiformal	Women wear elegant, shorter dresses (e.g., knee or tea length; minis are probably not appropriate). Men wear dark suits (or sport coat with dress pants), with or without a tie.
Black Tie	Men wear tuxedos. Ladies can wear long or shorter (knee-length) fancy dresses; floor-length gowns are not required.

(continued)

Dress Code	Description / Appropriate Attire
White Tie	The most formal category of dressing. Women should wear long, formal gowns. Men wear black tailcoats and black pants, a vest, shirt, and tie—all of which are white.
Black-Tie Optional	Men can wear either tuxes or dark suits with ties; ladies wear elegant dresses (long or short) or fancy separates (think sequins and beading).
Creative Black Tie	Same as black tie, but you can add some sort of particularly stylish element or trendy accessory.
"Resort" Casual	A dressy version of casual clothing. Think Bermuda shorts, summer shifts, and knit tops.

ness Yum Yum Chefs, Gracia built a career as a beauty publicist in New York City. At one point, after years as a publicity manager at Kiehl's, Gracia had just gotten a new job as the publicity director at Armani cosmetics and felt she had to "step it up" in terms of her clothing, since she was going to be at Armani. On the day she accepted the job, one of her new colleagues at Armani said they had an event that night at the Guggenheim and asked if Gracia could make it. "I was thinking to myself, 'Oh sh*t, what will I wear?' But I said of course I'd be there!" Gracia remembers. The Armani people didn't have enough time to call in something that she could borrow, so Gracia decided she would just go out and buy something Armani—because, as she says, this was her first impression! Gracia wasn't even sure what Armani clothes looked like, and she went to Saks and discovered there were multiple departments of the designer's clothes. "I asked the saleslady, what floor is Armani on, and she's like, 'Which label? Do you mean Black label? Colleccione?' and rattled off all these different lines. I didn't know!" Gracia found her way to the Colleccione department and eventually selected one dress and one pants-top outfit that cost a whopping $1,200 and $1,400, respectively!

Gracia reluctantly made the purchases, telling herself they were an "investment" and analyzing in her head their value over time, assuming she'd get a lot of use out of them that year (cost per wear!). But when she got home, she put on the dress again, looked in the mirror, and winced. "You could not even tell it was Armani," she says. "It was a basic, black matte-jersey dress—and it was not wowing me. I thought to myself, 'I'm never going to wear this thing again!'" As for the pants outfit? "It looked so bad, I knew I couldn't even take the tags off."

Gracia's boyfriend called, and, as she was approaching hysterics, she explained her conundrum. He advised

GGG PEARL:
On Dressing Up — A Few More Dos and Don'ts

- It's okay to wear a chic black dress to a wedding, but don't even consider wearing all white!
- Do take cues from an event's time and place. For example, an afternoon, outdoor wedding calls for a more casual yet festive dress (think florals), whereas a Saturday night, downtown city wedding means satin and glam.
- Don't wear a pair of heels that you can't walk or even stand in—no matter how cute they are!
- Do go stocking free if you're wearing open-toed, strappy sandals. To create smooth lines under a clingy ensemble, wear footless pantyhose or Power Panties from Spanx.
- If it's a work party, don't show too much skin. That means no backless gowns, and think *very carefully* about showing

(continued)

her to calm down and just put on something she already owned—that she had plenty of black items in her closet and that black always looks good! "I ended up pulling out this skirt from my closet that I'd bought on sale—it was a balloon-type black taffeta skirt with a pocket—and paired it with a $100 black top I had that was from Ann Taylor," Gracia says. "The outfit I ended up wearing maybe cost $200—and I got so many compliments on it that night!"

In fact, she was chatting with a guy who was dating a friend of hers at Kiehl's, and he ended up asking her to come interview for a job at the company where he worked—just because he "loved her look" that night! Says Gracia, "I know that if I'd worn that $1,400 outfit and felt like a dud, none of that would have happened."

Gracia's story reveals several key ideas: first, you can never underestimate the power of an extra-chic ensemble. Second, with a bit of creativity, getting glam absolutely does *not* have to cost a fortune. And finally, even when you're dressed up, it's critical that you feel comfortable and confident in what you're wearing. (How else will you feel bold enough to work the room?) Remember: when it comes to clothes, Go-Getter Girls are always appropriate—and selectively fabulous! Don't worry about looking perfect all the time, but be ready to release your inner GGG fashionista when the moment is right!

8

Natural Beauty Is Bullsh*t!!

*I*n March 2001, Oprah decided to "blow the cover" on all that it takes to get her visage on the front of *O* magazine each month. "So many women, myself included, see a magazine and think, 'Now, why don't *I* look like that?' Let's show everybody what being a cover girl really takes," was how she explained the idea. The article detailed all the decision making, primping, reshooting, and *nineteen wardrobe changes* it took—by at least a couple dozen crew members—to get Oprah looking camera ready. Between the lighting adjustments, industrial-strength wind machine, and makeup (including custom-blended foundation, layered lipstick shades, and Oprah's trademark false eyelashes) involved in the shoot, the article left many readers assured that what they saw in the final cover shot was more magic than reality. Toward the end of the shoot Oprah even joked that, Cinderella-like, her physical transformation would soon go *poof.* "My hair's good for one more hour," she warned. "My face is halfway back to Chicago."

If there is one thing that celebrity journalism has revealed to us (besides the unfortunate vajay-jay views of starlets who, despite loads of free clothes, can't seem to find a satisfactory pair of underwear!), it's that even the most gorgeous women in the world do not roll out of bed looking beautifully groomed and so-called picture-perfect. All you have to do is flip through one of those layouts with the headline screaming "Stars! They're just like us!" or "Celebrities! Without Makeup!" to see just how transformational top-notch hair and makeup can be and to feel a twinge of self-satisfaction that, yes, stars do have bags under their eyes, bushy eyebrows, and greasy hair or—the most unbelievable—bad skin! Granted, this bit of validation is probably fleeting because, just as soon as you turn the page—after having ogled the picture in detail to determine that the monster zit or cellulite was not in fact photoshopped into existence—you see the same actress or model done up for a movie premiere, and your notion that celeb beauty is just an illusion quickly congeals to its previous solid-state reality.

It's not as if celebrities themselves don't talk about this type of thing all the time. Kelly Ripa, for example, recently said that she wakes up looking like a "Chihuahua." Sarah Jessica Parker has admitted that she can't do a single thing to tame her curly hair besides whip it into a ponytail. Tyra Banks is known for talking about her hair weave, while Jessica Simpson is such a consumer of extensions that she now sells them! Courteney Cox—a self-proclaimed product junkie who confesses that she once overused Botox—is forthcoming about her exhaustive regimen because, as she shared in *Marie Claire* in November 2008, she thinks women should "be totally open with other women about what they do to make themselves look better." But somehow it's still too easy for most of us to forget that being "beautiful" can take some serious maintenance. Perhaps the disconnect is partly that we *do* know these movie stars and TV personalities go all out for their public appearances—but what's to explain that perfectly coifed pharmaceutical rep who you see strutting down the street looking straight out of a Cover Girl commercial? Surely—as a regular working woman—she doesn't have a squadron of beauty pros making her look good each morning. Well, Go-Getter Girls aren't so easily fooled! Let's demystify it once and for all.

From the Go-Getter Girl perspective, basically, natural beauty is bullsh*t! Go-Getter Girls know that any woman who looks totally pretty, put together, and polished—whether she's a star, a socialite, your colleague, your neighbor, or your friend—put multiple tiers of effort into her grooming and beauty rituals. Sure, there is that teensy percentage of women who wake up gloriously beautiful and require no primping or plucking to look fab (damn those freshly scrubbed Laguna Beach gals!). But for the rest of us out there—including zillions of famous, successful women—looking great requires a virtual brigade of hairstylists, colorists, waxers, aestheticians, nail technicians, and more. "It takes a village," as investment banker and GGG Ann Lawrence, age thirty-seven, from Miami, admits about her own beauty routine.

As with anything else, Go-Getter Girls know that being well-groomed does not happen by accident. There will be appointments, consultations, regimens, lotions, makeup, squeezing, pulling, shaving, conditioning, spraying, and, yes, sometimes a little pain (hello, Brazilians!). Accept this. Actually, embrace it. Isn't it liberating, in a way, to know that looking your personal best is something over which you do have a reasonable amount of control? Sure, you will likely be doing some variety of things that a "purist" could term "fake"—whether that means coloring your roots, straightening your hair, polishing your nails, lengthening your lashes, redefining your brows, or bronzing your skin. It's not fake; it's maintenance. Everyone knows that even guys only *say* they want "natural" beauty—that is, until you stop shaving your legs, armpits, and bikini line for three months!

While grooming is a top priority in the GGG repertoire, you don't need to—and shouldn't—spend all day or blow your entire rent or mortgage payment on your beauty regimen! You do, however, need to establish your personal beauty priorities—in terms of both the time and money you should invest in them. For example, GGG Phebe Neely, a senior manager at Deloitte who long ago made peace with her thick, curly hair, has never colored and rarely so much as trims her wash-and-go locks, but she religiously gets her eyebrows threaded. Or consider Maria Lopez,★ a thirty-four-year-old event planner from Michigan, who spends about three seconds slicking on some berry lip gloss each day but schedules her nail appointments as if they were business meetings. As Maria explains, she had reached a point in her career where she viewed this ritual as part of her job, not a luxury. She actually doesn't find sitting in the pedicure lounge chair relaxing anymore—especially because she is usually trying to multitask on her BlackBerry at the same time. "But it's just something you have to do," she says, "because you can't walk into a client meeting with chipped nails!" For GGG Donatella Arpaia, the glamorous owner of several top-rated restaurants, including Anthos, Mia Dona, KEFI, and Gus and Gabriel in Manhattan, and EDS in Miami, regular manis and pedis are also a "must," and, because she says she "stinks" at drying her own hair, a top priority is getting her hair blown out once or twice a week. "It's maintenance in my world," she says. However, given the frequency of these appointments, she doesn't break the bank each time. While she has her color and cut done at a swanky salon, she opts for quality cheapie blow-out spots where she gets her hair done for just $20 or $30.

As she allocates her beauty budget, a GGG must decide, for example, what is most noticeable in her profession (e.g., Maria's manicures); which products and services really "work" for her after years of trial and error; which services, such as highlights, are best done by a professional (to avoid mishaps); or what makes her feel most glamorous or refreshed when given a free hour for pampering. A GGG intent on having straight hair may be willing to dole out hundreds of bucks for the complicated Japanese thermal-reconditioning procedure because the relief from daily round-brush straightening is worth the cost, but to get her biweekly manicures at the budget salon on the corner. Or she may swear by a $10 drugstore moisturizer like Oil of Olay yet have nothing but Kérastase shampoo and conditioner in her shower and spend some big bucks to get her arms waxed at an upscale spa. You get the idea: you have to strategically determine what works for your budget, your style, and your schedule!

GGG WORKSHEET

We all have a finite amount of time, energy, and money to spend on primping. Begin to think strategically about your beauty regimen by ranking, in order, your top-five beauty priorities:

1. _____

2. _____

3. _____

4. _____

5. _____

In addition to being well-groomed, it's important to wear *at least a little makeup* in professional settings: studies show that this could affect your earning power. For example, a study published in the *Journal of Applied Social Psychology* revealed that women who wore cosmetics were associated with greater earning potential and considered to have more prestigious jobs—as well as perceived to be healthier and more confident—than women without cosmetics.

Interesting findings, right? But before the cosmetic-averse become overwhelmed, don't think you need to apply a "full face" of stage makeup. GGGs tend to wear just enough to give them a refreshed, healthy look. After all, isn't it the worst when a colleague comes up to you and says, "You look really *tired* today—are you okay?" A little concealer, lipstick or lip gloss, mascara, and maybe some blush go a long way! Need some help with the logistics? Get acquainted with the five following must-haves for a five-minute GGG makeup routine:

1. Concealer: First, dab a few dots of eye cream (preferably a light-consistency or gel-based option that easily absorbs) underneath your eye. Smooth in. Using a shade that is one or two shades lighter than your skin, apply concealer with a brush or fingertip under-

neath the eye, making sure to cover the area all the way over to the nose and inner corner of the eye and up to the lower lashes. Pat in to blend. Check out the results in natural light; apply another layer if needed.

2. Powder: Using a large powder brush, dust translucent or skin-matching powder under your eyes (to set concealer) and all over face (or simply areas that tend to shine, such as the T-zone).

3. Peachy-pink colored blush or bronzer: Apply color to blush brush and tap off excess. Smile! Apply blush mainly to apples of the cheeks and sweep upward toward the hairline. Blend. If using bronzer, dust onto cheekbones, forehead, and/or chin for a tawny glow.

4. Mascara: If you have straight lashes or want added oomph for naturally curled lashes, curl lashes with an eyelash curler. Then apply black mascara from the underside of top lashes, moving from the base of the lashes to tip, wiggling the brush side to side a little as you go. To keep your focus and get the most coverage of lashes, try applying while you look down into a mirror (instead of looking straight ahead); while holding your eyelid in place by pulling up gently at the eyebrow bone; or while forming your mouth in an O shape as you apply. Apply one or two coats to top lashes. Applying to lower lashes is optional; to do so, hold the brush vertically.

5. Lip gloss: Use a shade similar to your natural lip color. For a more glam look, try one with a bit of gold or silver shimmer in it. Apply straight from the tube (no separate brush is needed), covering both top and bottom lip.

GGG Guide:
Beauty Services Decoded

Ever wonder what your friend meant when she said her colorist was so great at balayage? (Hint: that means hand-painted highlights!) Check out the glossary-style primer below for some basic guidance on salon, spa, and medical services that you might incorporate into your GGG beauty regimen.

· **Artificial nails:** various methods of fortifying and adding length to your nails. Typical preparations involve acrylic (for tips), acrylic gel overlays, or silk wraps. Because they can weaken natural nails, artificial nails (and especially tips) have fallen out of favor. The look these days is a natural nail, kept at a shorter, elegant length. (Think just past the end of the fingertip.)

· **Balayage:** a hair-highlighting technique in which the color is hand-painted onto hair with a sweeping motion. Results can be more natural looking and less methodical than traditional foil highlights.

· **Bikini wax:** warm or cool wax is applied to the bikini line and ripped away once it sets to remove the hair. (You're usually wearing a pair of paper panties.) Hair must be about a quarter-inch long for it to grip. It is not exactly a pleasant sensation—less so if done a few days before or after your period, when bloating makes hair more difficult to grip. Minimize pain by popping an ibuprofen an hour before your appointment or by using a numbing cream.

· **Blow-out:** hair is washed and professionally blown dry and styled at a salon.

Body scrub or body polish: an exfoliating scrub is carefully applied to your whole body, then rinsed off, and lotion is massaged in / applied.

Body wrap: skin is exfoliated, then some type of detoxifying mask is applied all over (and in some instances, you are then wrapped like a mummy in warm towels or some type of heat-conducting material). Claims to improve skin elasticity or reduce cellulite. Usually turns out to be an uncomfortable, sticky mess.

Botox: trade name for botulinum toxin type A. Contains a neurotoxin protein in tiny amounts to paralyze nerves when injected into skin, for the purpose of temporarily eliminating wrinkles (e.g., furrowed brow). Also used in the armpits to treat excessive sweating (it really works) and even in the soles of feet to better facilitate stiletto wearing.

Brazilian bikini wax: a bikini wax where the technician also removes the hair in between the butt cheeks and the hair on most or all of the vulva as well (yikes!), depending on preference (some leave a "landing strip"). Usually the waxer will use a cooler, hard, Brazilian-style wax that is peeled off with bare fingers instead of cloth strips.

Bronzer: a powder or gel makeup that is applied to skin to create a tawny, sun-kissed glow and to highlight areas of the face.

Deep conditioner: helps repair or protect damaged hair. An ultrahydrating concoction is applied to hair either at home or in the salon and left on for several minutes. Hair is usually covered with some type of plastic cap and/or you sit under a dryer to allow full penetration. Salon versions may contain

(continued)

some sort of oil and protein; DIY recipes may contain icky things like mayonnaise, beer, avocado, or eggs.

· Depilator: cream, such as Nair or Veet, that contains chemicals to remove hair at the surface of skin. Always test a strand first. Some people have allergic reactions to these creams.

· Dermabrasion: a process by which a technician (typically medically trained) uses sandpaper or some other mechanical substance to remove the top layers of skin and improve skin's texture and appearance. For example, it is used to buff away acne scars or fine wrinkles.

· Electrolysis: permanent hair-removal technique where a small needle is inserted into each hair follicle to deliver a zap that cauterizes the root. Requires multiple treatments; feels like a series of static-electricity shocks.

· Exfoliate: a granular substance (such as sugar or salt) or an alpha-hydroxy acid (such as lactic or glycolic acid) is used to gently slough off dead skin cells.

· Extractions: process by which blackheads or whiteheads are removed from skin during a facial. Can be tricky to do correctly, and painful even when done so. Make sure the aesthetician is properly licensed and trained.

· Facial: skin-clarifying treatment that involves some combination of cleansing, exfoliating, steaming, as well as the application of a deep-cleansing or hydrating mask and moisturizer. At a spa, it usually involves a massage of the shoulders and neck as well.

- Flat iron: process that takes sections of hair and runs them through clamped hot plates; used to reduce frizz and make hair silky. Experts believe ceramic irons are less damaging to the hair than metal.

- Hair color: multiple options exist to change or freshen your natural shade and add shine. Generally speaking, in order from most to least chemicals, there's permanent color, semipermanent color, demipermanent or deposit-only color, or color "glaze." For best results, consult a professional.

- Hair extensions: a variety of methods to add length and volume to hair. Can be temporary, such as clip-in pieces, or semipermanent, where hair is either sewn in (to cornrows of your natural hair) or bonded/fused to the end of natural hair. Can be made from synthetic or human hair.

- Highlights: typically foils are used to separate thin or thick chunks of hair and dye them a color that is both lighter than your base color or natural shade and complementary to your skin tone.

- Japanese thermal-conditioning treatment: a straightening procedure marketed mainly to Caucasian and Asian women. A solution of diluted ammonium thioglycolate is applied, then hair is dried and flat-ironed to change the hair structure. Cost ranges from $300 to $700 or more!

- Laser hair removal: laser light targets the melanin in your hair to permanently inhibit growth. Requires multiple sessions. Works best for people with light skin and dark hair. Said to be less painful than electrolysis and to feel like a rubber band snapping against skin.

(continued)

- **Lash extensions:** semipermanent eyelash extensions are glued (by a certified technician) to the ends of your own. Last four to six weeks. Can be expensive and tricky to wear. For a glam night out, just try some standard fake lashes from the drugstore!

- **Layering:** haircut that involves cutting layers into hair to create interest and swing. Method reached fever-pitch popularity when *Friends* star Jennifer Aniston debuted her signature updated-shag Rachel do in the '90s. Lately, the look for layers is more subtle, like "long" layers or just some angling around the face.

- **Lowlights:** same as highlights, but chunks of hair are dyed a shade that is darker than your natural shade. Often used in conjunction with one or more colors of highlights to create a more natural, blended, multidimensional result.

- **Manicure:** fingernail-grooming procedure that involves shaping, filing, and buffing nails; grooming cuticles; and applying polish. Most experts recommend not cutting your cuticles. When it comes to polish, go for pale pink or beige nudes to make chips inconspicuous. If you like brights (e.g., red, coral), know these colors only look modern and chic on short nails.

- **Parrafin-wax treatment:** helps soften and exfoliate skin. Heated paraffin wax is placed on (typically) hands or feet, then covered with some type of plastic or glove, allowed to cool, and peeled off.

- **Pedicure:** toenail- and foot-grooming procedure that involves shaping and cleaning nails; sloughing off of dead skin with a pumice-type stone—avoid the razor—calf massage/exfoliation; and toenail-polish application. Make sure all tools used are completely sterile.

- Relaxer: cream concoction of chemicals is applied to hair to straighten it. Used primarily on African-American or ultracurly ethnic hair.

- Self-Tanner: a lotion that contains the chemical dihydroxyacetone (DHA), which darkens the skin. Many varieties are available for face and body, including everyday body lotions like Jergen's Natural Glow. To avoid streaky or orange finish, experts suggest exfoliating before application.

- Spray tan or airbrush tan: a self-tanning solution is sprayed onto the body while you stand, either by a machine (e.g., Mystic Tan) or by an actual person wielding an airbrush spray can that looks kind of like a blowtorch. A proper airbrush tan has been known to create the illusion of cleavage or ab definition on celebs.

- Sun protection: ideally, daily use of a moisturizer or lotion with an SPF 15. When major sun exposure is expected, experts recommend using sunblock of at least SPF 30 and using a shot glass full of lotion for each allover-body application.

- Teeth whitening: a peroxide solution is applied to teeth to whiten them about three to ten shades, depending on method/concentration of peroxide. Can be done at the dentist's office, or at home using take-home trays or drugstore-bought strips (such as Crest Whitestrips). In-office procedures offer the most accelerated and dramatic results, but at-home treatments—if done for the recommended time period—can be very effective.

(continued)

> **Threading:** ancient Eastern process of hair removal, through which a technician manipulates two strands of thread to loop around and remove hairs. Used mainly for the face (e.g., brows, upper lip, chin). Some women prefer threading to waxing because there is no burn potential, and it may cause less irritation.
>
> **Waxing:** hair-removal technique in which warm wax is applied to the unwanted hair, then a cloth strip is pressed on top and ripped away, taking the wax and hair with it. Can be performed on both the face and body. Not recommended for people with certain skin conditions or using certain medications (e.g., Retin-A or Accutane). Check with your doctor.

If you need help with choosing colors and application tips, grab a makeup-minded relative or friend and head to a trusted department store counter for a mini-makeover. You don't have to buy everything the consultant selects for you; it's customary to purchase one or two items—but you'll probably get a wealth of how-to knowledge if you pay attention and ask questions during the application process. Also, nowadays, many cosmetics companies, such as Bobbi Brown, Chanel, or Sephora, have great online tutorials—with videos! While some of us may never become experts at the tricky stuff (e.g., the illusive "three-dimensional" eye), you can follow along using your own products and become a pro at applying the basics in no time.

Finally, a quick note on the whole drugstore versus department-store beauty products: countless magazine articles and television segments have been devoted to this topic, and most of the time the experts conclude that the cost of a department store product is in the packaging, whereas the "active ingredients" in the expensive and cheapie products are often the same. This may be true, but most luxury-brand devotees will never be so easily convinced! I know one GGG who swears up and down on the $125-per-ounce face cream by La Mer—whose parent company, Estée Lauder, has actually been sued for false advertising by women saying they were duped by La Mer's Miracle Broth promises. (One of the cream's main ingredients, btw, is petrolatum—essentially, Vaseline!) On the other hand, GGG Keri Glassman is a celebrity nutritionist, nutrition contributor to *Women's Health* magazine and CBS's *The Early Show,* and a health and beauty entrepreneur whose skin-care line, Skin Appétit, is sold at RiteAid and Walgreens, and she says she's always been a devout drugstore beauty girl. "I remember my mom bought me a tube of Shiseido eye cream when I was thirteen, but besides that, I've used Olay and Lubriderm lotions and Dove soap to wash my face and body, my entire life!"

There are many mainstay drugstore items that even pros swear go

GGG PEARL:
On Contouring

So you're not totally keen on your profile. Here's a makeup contouring trick that Tyra Banks has shared with many a supermodel. It takes just a few minutes—and it really works!

- Start with a concealer that matches your skin or is one shade lighter.
- Squeeze out a dab on your finger and begin tracing a line down the bridge of your nose—the straightest part.
- Keeping with the same vertical line, put a dab on the front of your chin and also on your forehead.
- Blend in—the idea being that you are trying to create one continuous (but imperceptible) line from forehead to chin.
- You'll also want to make sure to apply concealer under the eyes and blend well.
- Set with a dusting of translucent powder (MAC and Bobbi Brown are faves).

toe-to-toe with any expensive brand, such as Cetaphil cleanser and Maybelline Great Lash mascara. But overall, it really just depends on the particular product, your beauty needs, and your preferences. There is something so glam about those glossy gold-and-black Chanel boxes, isn't there? One rule of thumb: consult magazines that do comparisons, roundups, and readers'-choice awards for the best drugstore beauty products, such as *Self*, *Allure*, *InStyle*, *Women's Health*, and *Good Housekeeping*. Let the beauty editors and experts discern the winners from the losers—this way, you can avoid reliving your seventh-grade experiments with Wet n Wild lipstick and St. Ives Apricot Scrub!

It may take some trial and error to nail down your beauty regimen, but with a little effort, a bit of knowledge, and some key beauty tricks, you'll be able to put your best, beautiful face forward—and get on with your fabulous Go-Getter Girl day! One more note: even though you'll no longer be fooled by the ubiquitous airbrushed media images of so-called "natural" beauties, there's no reason why you also can't embrace some of the secrets of celebrity beautifiers. Below, nine great tips from beauty insiders:

1. Mally Roncal, who is J.Lo and Beyonce's go-to makeup gal, believes that less can be more: don't use base unless you need it. In fact, the first time she did Beyonce's makeup, she finished in fifteen minutes! "I just couldn't bring myself to put foundation on her flawless skin," she has said. (Source: *Marie Claire,* October 2005.)

2. Ted Gibson, hair guru to the likes of Angelina Jolie, recommends washing hair only once every two days or longer. As he told vanity fair.com in December 2008, "Less frequent washing is one of the easiest ways to keep hair healthy, and it doesn't cost a thing!"

3. Deborah Lippmann, celebrity manicurist who has groomed the digits of everyone from Oprah to Sarah Jessica Parker, recommends filing nails from the outer edge to the center using a medium-grade black file (not emery or metal, which can cause nails to split). And she suggests keeping nail polish in the refrigerator: it will last longer. (Source: lippmanncollection.com.)

4. Ken Paves, who is Jessica Simpson's and Eva Longoria's mane man, is a big fan of the ponytail. As he shared with InStyle.com, you can look effortlessly chic by first curling one-inch sections of hair, then teasing the crown slightly, and pulling hair back into a ponytail. Or, you can wear a high ponytail—to highlight cheekbones.

5. Facialist to stars such as Gisele and Hilary Swank, Christine Chin, who is known for deep-digging skin treatments, says to never use a washcloth to wash your face. "Hands are better—you always know that they're clean." (Source: *Allure*, February 2007.)

6. Exclusive brow specialist Sania Vucetaj says that if you must touch up brows between appointments, look in a regular mirror (i.e., not the magnifying kind) and tweeze only the strays underneath the arch. Her favorite tweezers? Tweezerman, slant tip. (Sources: harpers bazaar.com; oprah.com.)

7. Colorist extraordinaire Rita Hazan, whose client roster includes Heidi Klum, Halle Berry, and Gwyneth Paltrow, recommended on *Oprah*'s "Great American Haircut" episode (November 2007), that you can try a salon or drugstore glossing treatment once a month to prevent color from fading.

8. Kate Somerville, skin saver of celebs such as Jessica Alba and Debra Messing, recommends applying moisturizer the second you get out of the tub or shower to lock in moisture. (Source: *Allure*, February 2007.)

9. Hairstylist Clyde Haygood, who has worked with Gwen Stefani and Andie MacDowell, said to *InStyle* that dryer sheets are a great way to subdue frizzies. Just run a sheet over your hair and flyaway strands are tamed in an instant.

As you begin to develop your own beauty regimen, think of it as one more tool in your GGG arsenal to help give you a little confidence boost and establish your polished presence. Remember, don't feel as if you can never leave the house without lipstick! I know one GGG cosmetics executive who says she doesn't worry much about how she looks just running errands at Home Depot, but when she does get made up, she puts some thought into it. "Even if I decide to wear a new lip color at a meeting with one of our retailers, I probably did that with the intention of convincing them to carry that shade!" she says. "I don't just put on makeup 'just because.' I know why I do it! I know the outcome, and I do it with purpose." In sum, as a GGG, be as intentional and strategic about your look as you would other areas of your life and career—and don't apologize for taking care of yourself. As those famous L'Oréal commercials say, "You're worth it!"

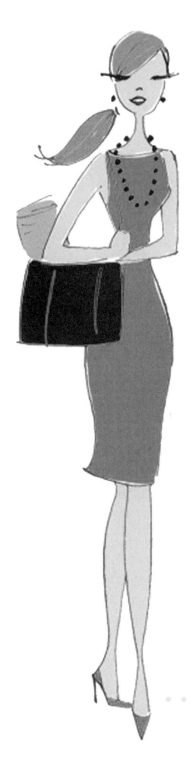

Part Three

HOW TO GET AHEAD!

9.

The Best Education
Is Self-Education

*N*ow that you've got the mind-set and looks of a Go-Getter Girl, let's get down to work-world specifics. The road of office life can be rocky, so you'll need some key strategies for handling common career conundrums. First and foremost, Go-Getter Girls know that the best education is self-education. Remember Peter B. Kyne's parable *The Go-Getter*, which I first mentioned in part one? In that tale, the main character, lumber salesman Bill Peck, who is eager to prove his mettle, must purchase a blue vase and deliver it to his boss, Cappy Ricks. Sounds easy enough, but this simple task turns out to be the mother of all errands when his boss secretly sabotages the hunt for the vase with various obstacles—continually changing the name on the storefront, posting a police-man outside the door to keep him from breaking the window to get the vase, and pricing the vase at such an exorbitant amount that Peck must dig up thousands of dollars (in a town where he knows no one) to buy it. Amazingly, Peck jumps through all the hoops and catches an already-departed train to hand the boss the vase, at which point the boss reveals that it was all a setup, what Cappy Ricks calls the "Degree of the Blue Vase," which is Ricks's "supreme test for a go-getter." Over the years, Ricks says, only three of the thirty men assigned the task emerged victorious. For his triumph, Peck is awarded a coveted management position in Shanghai. Ricks says that the "[The Degree of the Blue Vase] is a job that many before you have walked away from at the first sign of an obstacle. You thought you carried into this stateroom a two-thousand-dollar vase, but between ourselves, what you really carried in was a ten-thousand-dollar job as our Shanghai manager."

Peck, a former soldier, explains to the boss why he didn't quit, citing his old brigade motto, "It shall be done." "If any officer in his brigade showed signs of flunking his job because it appeared impossible," says Peck, "the brigadier would just look at him once—and then that officer would remember the motto and go and do his job or die trying."

Okay, so the story is obviously a little extreme, with its brigadier-espoused life-and-death lingo and all! But it definitely contains a lesson that will ring true to any modern-day Go-Getter Girl. The moral of the story—"It shall be done"—is basically a way of saying that employers don't have time to hold your hand, and the employees who impress and succeed are those who can teach themselves how to get stuff done (or find the people who can help teach them) with very little direction. Think about Meryl Streep's character Miranda Priestly (a thinly veiled portrait of *Vogue* magazine priestess Anna Wintour) in the recent hit movie *The Devil Wears Prada*. Miranda is all about giving little tests to her new assistants. She starts out by assigning menial tasks like hanging up her coat and handbags, fetching her lattes ten times a day, or producing a piping hot steak on demand (which she then claims she doesn't want!). Once an assistant has proved herself, she can move "up the ladder" to the more important errand of delivering the "book"—a daily mock-up of that month's magazine issue—to Miranda's apartment at night.

When the main character in the movie, a non-fashion-minded young woman named Andy, messes up some travel arrangements, Miranda issues her own version of the Degree of the Blue Vase: she gives Andy the task of procuring the *unpublished* manuscript of the newest Harry Potter book for her twin daughters by that afternoon—and it's clear that Andy's job depends on it! So what does Andy do? She starts hustling! She's racing around town, calling every contact she can think of, and she eventually calls on a writer-friend who knows someone who knows someone who has the manuscript. When the clock strikes 3 P.M., Miranda is sure Andy will have failed the insurmountable obstacle, but Andy has already delivered the copies—two of them, and bound!—to Miranda's daughters, who are enjoying the pursuits of Harry on their train ride to Grandma's. Miranda is stunned (or maybe not), and not only is Andy's job intact, but the triumph earns her Miranda's trust, and Andy starts to get the plum assignments.

While not every boss will purposely throw you to the wolves like Miranda Priestly or the boss in *The Go-Getter*, Go-Getter Girls take it upon themselves to *become* a wolf—in chic clothing, of course. At work you will be rewarded for figuring out a way to get something done—and this often has little to do with book smarts or your educational background. As one Go-Getter Girl put it, "I really loved college—but college doesn't necessarily teach you anything in terms of practical skills." Carving a path to success in the work world is all about *self*-education and being resourceful: going online to figure out everything there is to know about a topic your boss is curious about, calling up a dozen industry movers and shakers to familiarize yourself with a new reporting beat, ravenously seeking out information to be the most knowledgeable person in the room on that potential client your company is trying to land, thinking about a solution to a problem before consulting your boss for advice, or becoming an expert in an area you maybe knew nothing about. That, in a nutshell, is the Go-Getter Girl path to success! Moreover, remember that when you are first starting out in a field, no task is too menial for you to begin to build the relevant practical skills. Often, junior-level employees may have to compromise and take on tasks that they don't want to do in order to attain the positions where they have more freedom and more autonomy. If you are resourceful enough to figure out and master the "small" stuff, the big stuff will come your way, trust me.

GGG Nugget of Wisdom: *Having a degree from a great school won't hurt you, but when it comes to making it in the real world, you have to be resourceful and figure out a way to solve problems, despite obstacles.*

Consider the incredible story of Go-Getter Girl Sara Blakely, founder of the Spanx line of undergarments. Before she was the gal who got our "butts covered"—as the Spanx motto goes—Sara made her living as a fax-machine saleswoman and stand-up comedian. A lover of fashionable clothes, though not actually trained in fashion or design, she was frustrated by her visible thong and the little bit of jiggle beneath her favorite lightweight, unlined cream pants. So one day, as the story goes, she cut off the bottoms of her pantyhose, put them on underneath the pants, and discovered butt-smoothing, panty-line-free results with an unfortunate side effect: the pantyhose rolled up her legs all night.

Sara was convinced she had a blockbuster on her hands. So what did she do? She went online and taught herself everything there is to know about the intricate topic of textiles. Using trial and error, she took elements—waistband and panty and crotch—of all her favorite hosiery, and spent weeks coming up with a combo of nylon and Lycra that was comfortable. Once she figured out a way to make the hose stay put, she went to the library after work every night and taught herself how to write a patent and trademark the product—even though she had zero legal training. She actually spent hours, days, *years* trying to come up with a name for her invention, polling friends and family and drawing on her previous experiences in comedy and marketing: Sara knew from doing stand-up that crowds respond to the *k* sound; she knew that the most recognized brands in the world, such as Coca-Cola and Kodak, also featured the *k* sound. She ultimately chose to spell her product's name *Spanx* with an *x*, instead of *Spanks* with a *k*, because, as she learned through research, made-up names are easier to trademark.

Next, Sara had to get the product made, and, sure enough, she was rejected by every single factory she called. She eventually got in her car and drove around North Carolina for a week begging manufacturers to make her invention, the footless pantyhose. Finally, one manufacturer "got" her idea—"He called me back and told me he would make the hose because his two daughters thought it was brilliant," she says.

It took about a year to perfect the prototype. Then, with a bona fide sample in hand, Sara begged for a ten-minute meeting with a Neiman Marcus buyer and flew to Dallas. "I literally brought her into the ladies' room with me, got butt naked, took my prototype Spanx out of a Ziploc bag, and tried them on underneath my pants," Sara says. "The buyer took one look at the results and said, 'You're in!'" Three weeks later, Spanx were on the shelves of Neiman Marcus. After being blessed with a kiss from Oprah—who named Spanx one of her "favorite things" in 2000—her sales started to take off and rose rapidly; a business that began with $5,000 in savings surpassed $350 million in retail sales in 2008 alone. Spanx, and its even more affordable sister line, Assets, now offer dozens of smartly packaged undergarments that are adored by celebrities from Gwyneth to Tyra to Teri. Yet Sara, who considers herself an accidental inventor, had neither design nor legal training; she self-educated her way to success.

In fact, Sara is constantly educating herself about what women want and need in their undergarments. Each new Spanx product is born from months' worth of requests from women, many of which come in the form of e-mails that say things like "Please tell Sara to put a foot on Spanx—winter's coming." She gets input from her "focus group"—her mom and her grandma—as well as the dozens of fashion-minded women who populate the Spanx office, one of whom lamented the line socks left on her calves (aha! the topless trouser sock!). Sara, a former saleswoman without any kind of fashion, legal, or advanced degree, self-educated her way to being an award-winning inventor/designer, and, oh yeah, a millionaire several times over!

How does the self-education lesson translate to the typical corporate setting? First, remember that when you arrive at a new workplace, it will take you a little while to learn the ins and outs of the office. To do this, sometimes it's better to listen more than you talk. As my dad used to say, that's the reason why you have two ears and one mouth! By listening and paying attention, you will begin to absorb who and what is important—such as what types of ideas the company values, which managers are the movers and shakers, and which projects will put you on the fast track. Remember, though, it needs to be *active* listening. As Go-Getter Girl Bonnie Fuller has said, "You need to have your antennae up."

GGG Nugget of Wisdom: *When you enter a new work environment, you can begin to self-educate by osmosis. Listen more than you talk but make sure that your "radar" is on to gather information about how you can succeed.*

For example, when Bonnie Fuller first started at *Women's Wear Daily*, the trade publication that is the bible of the fashion industry, she didn't have a clue about what she could do to impress her bosses. To be honest, she wasn't even thinking about that; for the first several months, she was just focused on completing her basic job requirements. But she was paying attention during editorial meetings and staff discussions, and soon she began to absorb—as if by osmosis, she says—the key areas her bosses could use her help with. She clicked in to what would enable her to "make a statement" in her editors' eyes. "I saw that they were constantly talking about or concerned about the covers or this particular spread in the middle of the magazine or finding trendy or newsy bits," she says. "That's when I started to focus. I thought, 'Oh, I can get better pics for this spread' or 'I've got to keep my eyes out for the hot trend.' I started to clue in on the types of information I needed to gather and present to my editors." Once Bonnie began to understand what was needed in her workplace, she was able to step up and volunteer more, which paved the way for her success at the magazine.

GGG Nugget of Wisdom: *Depth can be better than breadth. While it's good to have a base of knowledge on a variety of topics, your golden success opportunity might arise by becoming the "go-to expert" on a very narrow subject.*

Now, let's say that you get your first big break at work. For example, you're given a project to develop ideas for a new ad campaign or business venture. A Go-Getter Girl doesn't depend on her supervisor to teach her all the ins and outs of the industry. She immerses herself completely in the subject matter to become an expert on her own. Consider Go-Getter Girl (and my college roommate) Jenn Hyman, introduced in chapter 1. Jenn was working at Starwood, the major hotel and resort corporation, doing strategic planning. She'd seen how well the company recognized customers for their business travel, but she observed that it didn't yet have customized programs for different types of leisure travel, so she had a hunch that a potential new area of business for the company was in wedding and honeymoon services. Jenn, then age twenty-three, was not married, nor was she one of those girls who has pored over wedding magazines since age eight in preparation for the big day. But Jenn knew she needed to become an "expert" in everything weddings in order to pitch her idea to her bosses.

Jenn started immersing herself by purchasing every single wedding magazine and reading it cover to cover. She studied the structure, content, and function of wedding Web portals such as theknot.com and weddingchannel .com—and even worked up the nerve to call the CEO of weddingchannel .com and asked him to meet with her to discuss the industry. She researched wedding statistics and demographics to learn average wedding costs and how couples allocate their wedding budgets. She spoke with famous wedding planners such as David Tutera (the New York–based lifestyle expert extraordinaire who planned Star Jones's megawedding) and Mindy Weiss (the Los Angeles–based planner who's done the weddings of countless celebs from Andre Agassi to Reba McEntire). She also spoke with brides about what they wanted from a travel company and if they thought that any particular hotels were doing a good job already. Jenn lived, ate, and breathed weddings for weeks before she had educated herself enough to make the pitch to her bosses: a complete wedding-focused venture, which would include an online honeymoon registry that allowed couples to browse and create their ideal honeymoon at a Starwood hotel or resort. Wedding guests could even go online to give gifts like spa treatments toward the couple's honeymoon.

Because they were extremely impressed with Jenn's complete knowledge of the ins and outs of the wedding industry—not to mention her recommendations for innovative products such as a wedding concierge service—her bosses were sold instantly. At just twenty-three-years old, Jenn became one of the youngest entrepreneurs in the history of Starwood. She was given a staff and a budget of $750,000 to finance the program, which ended up grossing $13.5 million in its first year. Of course, Jenn got a big promotion and fatty raise, but what does every woman in the world want more than anything else? Jenn ended up being a guest on *The Oprah Winfrey Show* to give away honeymoons to runners-up on "Oprah's Million-Dollar Wedding Giveaway" show.

With the incredible access we have to media and the Internet, self-educating yourself to expert status on any given topic is not as hard as it might seem. The key is to immerse yourself in the topic. Some simple ways to self-educate include the following:

Ask questions. An easy way to learn more about something is simply to ask. Your boss or colleagues will often have more experience and knowledge, and a factoid that will take you hours to uncover might be on the tip of their tongues. Just remember: you might want to have done some preliminary research (see the next tip!) before you present your questions. Your boss will be more impressed with a well-thought-out, well-edited query.

Get to know Google. What did we all do before Google? Hands down the best research tool around, Google should be your first stop when you are clueless about anything.

Try the "one good case" method. When you're trying to learn everything there is to know about a new topic, it's easy to get overwhelmed. Find one good article or source of information and start building from there. In law school, this method is called "one good case." Basically, if you have a complex legal issue to figure out, the best way to approach it is to take the one case you know on the topic and read it to find the citations of more cases to read, and so on and so on. Eventually, the cases will all refer back to one another, and you'll realize not only that you've exhausted the resources on the issue but also that you've got a solid understanding of the subject matter.

Diversify your book and magazine shelf. As mentioned in chapter 3, Go-Getter Girls stay up on news and pop culture. But to gain perspective, make sure you consume a variety of media. Go-Getter Girls don't limit themselves to any one type of reading material. On any given day, for example, a Go-Getter Girl's magazine shelf might include *Vogue*, *The New Yorker*, *The Economist*, *Runner's World*, *Vibe*, and *Psychology Today*. In addition, many Go-Getter Girls read not only for education but also for inspiration. Go-Getter Girls interviewed cited everything from *The Prophet* by Khalil Gibran and *The Art of War* by Sun Tzu to *Unlimited Power* by Tony Robbins and *Work in Progress* by Michael Eisner as books that have helped motivate and guide them as they pursued their dreams. Step outside your reading "comfort zone" (and mix up your "favorites" list on Yahoo!), and you'll absorb new information to broaden your perspective—plus, you'll have interesting tidbits to discuss with colleagues and friends.

Watch some TV. Sure, we expect to be edified by *Meet the Press* or PBS, but who says you can't also learn a lot from watching reality television? Some shows (*Amazing Race*, anyone?) offer incredible insights into human behavior and serve as great conversation starters and water-cooler chatter. Certain shows can also legitimately teach you some vocabulary and fundamentals of your career field. In law school, our evidence professor encouraged us to watch *Law & Order* weekly!

Take a tour, virtual or real-world. Don't underestimate the teaching power of a guided tour, whether it's through a complicated software program or a fine-art museum. I once took a tour of downtown Chicago and in less than two hours became a veritable expert in modern and postmodern architecture.

Start dialing. While the Internet can be great, sometimes you learn more by just picking up the phone and having an actual conversation with someone. Think about it: good reporters don't rely on someone else's copy to develop their story. They get on the phone to get the story from the horse's mouth—and they talk to multiple sources to gain perspective and understanding. To familiarize yourself with a new topic or industry, identify at least three movers and shakers and ask them for insight.

Hit the library. It's almost an antiquated notion these days, but there are some topics that are best researched by looking in actual three-dimensional books! Plus, there's something about just being in a library that will make you feel almost glamorously smart and studious. Chances are you'll feel compelled to engross yourself in *learning* a lot more than if you're just sitting idly at a desk clicking your mouse.

Take a class—in anything. Whether it's bikram yoga, cooking, or Cantonese, developing a specialized area of knowledge will allow you to bring something new and different to the table. You never know when your "niche" will open the door to coveted opportunities.

GGG Nugget of Wisdom: *If you're willing to do the research, you can unearth amazing opportunities and experiences.*

Even when you are outside the work world and classroom, if you self-educate by simply doing a little bit of research, you can open up new doors and opportunities that you may not have even known existed. Go-Getter Girl Esther Pan, a Rhodes Scholarship finalist, *Newsweek* reporter-turned-playwright, and now, in her midthirties, a U.S. diplomat, became a pro at unearthing fellowships, scholarships, and, well, free money during her days as an undergrad at Stanford. After visiting a friend in Hawaii during her sophomore year, she paid a visit to the school's Undergraduate Research Programs Office, which would basically give students a sizable grant if they could come up with a worthy project. So Esther wrote up a twenty-page proposal about a play she was interested in doing, and, as she describes it, poof, they gave her $2,500. "It was great," says Esther. "I fell in love with Hawaii and surfed every day!"

Esther's Hawaii experience proved to be a lesson in "self-education" on two levels: first, she had the initiative to do the research to make the opportunity happen. Second, once she was there, her education was the *opposite* of a textbook experience. For the first few weeks in her new environment, she says she was just sort of "lost." She started taking night classes in Hawaiian language and going to the library to check out books but felt like she wasn't really gaining a lot of knowledge about Hawaiian culture.

Because Esther really didn't want to waste any of her precious time in Hawaii, she shifted her self-education strategy. "I realized, okay, I've committed to this place for three months, so I better do something to get the most out of this experience." Okay, that epiphany is part of the story—here's the rest: "Then I met a guy and just started hanging out with him!" The guy became her first great love and ended up being a perfect companion to explore Hawaii with. And spending time with him and his family allowed her to get more integrated into Hawaiian society. "By the end of the summer, I had learned so much more about culture by *not* taking classes," Esther says. Using her reporter's training—and the belief that people are usually willing to share their knowledge with you—she started talking to random people she encountered, including an old man on the beach. "I just went up to him and asked him to tell me what stories he had learned growing up in Hawaii. He told me about Pele, a goddess in Hawaiian mythology—and that story became the basis for my play."

In addition, the proposal-writing experience itself proved invaluable and inspired Esther to apply for "a million other things," including a grant to produce the play she wrote in Hawaii when she returned to Stanford her senior year; the Rhodes; and a Fulbright (she was awarded a creative fellowship, which took her to South Africa to complete a theater degree). "Most people don't know how to take advantage of these resources out there," she says.

Well, as you know, Go-Getter Girls aren't "most people"! They find a way to use the wealth of information and resources available to help them get ahead. Remember, the key is to have an open mind—be open to learning new ideas, trying new things, and experiencing new adventures. In work and in play, your ability to research will reap many rewards. So get out there and get (self-) educated!

10.

Cultivate Mentors

*G*GG Becky Green,★ a twenty-five-year-old from Austin, Texas, knew since she was about five years old that one day she wanted to open a clothing boutique. She went to college and tried some internships in advertising, but her heart wasn't in it. "I knew I wouldn't be happy until I was interacting with people all day and not behind a desk—and where I was the boss, where I was calling the shots!" she says. So how did she get going on making her boutique dream a reality? "I moved to Chicago for a year and became an 'intern' for a friend of mine from college, Samantha, who [had] just opened a boutique there and was doing very well." Samantha showed Becky how to run a business, mentoring her on everything from bookkeeping to buying to merchandising. "She really taught me everything I needed to know," says Becky. "She was just so kind—shared all of her knowledge—even opened up her accounting books!" After returning to Texas with all of her new insight, Becky literally went straight to market, and a year later she opened a boutique that now is one of the most popular shopping destinations in the city. "I never would have been able to do this without Samantha taking me under her wing," she says.

In a Go-Getter Girl career, mentors will play numerous roles, from friends who can coach you on the play-by-play of a new business to senior managers who help train you in your profession to powerful business leaders who can provide insight on the big-picture trajectory of your career. What exactly is a *mentor*? A mentor is someone who gives you *guidance* as you navigate your professional career—as one GGG puts it, "Somebody who can give you very pointed and specific advice at a certain point in your life." For example, you have an offer for job A and an offer for job B, and you call your mentor to ask which job he or she would recommend. Or you are just starting in a new profession, and there's a colleague a few levels up who helps you develop the skills or trains you on software or equipment that you need to do your job. However, as one GGG points out, "Your mentor is usually not going to be the person who *gives* you a job!"

Moreover, while you may develop "friend" mentors like Becky Green did, many of your mentors will hold a unique place in your network of advisers—and they are not necessarily your chums. GGG Soledad O'Brien, of CNN, believes that despite so much being written about mentoring, many young people misunderstand the nature of such a relationship. "I think a lot of people think they want mentors who can sit with them and guide them and hold their hand and chitchat. I can't do that! I don't have time for that. I want to do that with my kids and my husband," says Soledad. "A mentor is not like your girlfriend who you call up and say, 'Oh, I had the worst day today!'" Soledad has had many mentors and mentees whom she has hung on to for years, and she gets asked to be a mentor all the time, but sometimes she has to decline those requests if, for example, an up-and-coming journalist needs practical training or "hands-on care" that is beyond what she can offer. "I say to them, 'You know, I can't be your mentor, but here's my e-mail address, and if you have a specific question, feel free to e-mail me.' I can help them a little bit, but I can't be their sit-down, 'girlfriend' mentor." She thinks that in many instances, she can't really give them the skills and day-by-day guidance they need at that point in their career. "They don't need me—they need someone where they are, someone in their own workplace, that can help them," she says.

GGG Nugget of Wisdom: *You need to cultivate workplace mentors who help provide practical instruction and skills and longer-term mentors, who advise on major career decisions. Know the difference.*

To further explain, workplace mentors are the people who show you the ropes in your profession. For example, GGG Emily Oster, the University of Chicago economics professor who splashed onto the academic scene in her mid-twenties with her thought-provoking doctoral thesis on women, HIV, and hepatitis, says that in the academic world, much of the guidance a new professor needs from mentors is almost like "vocational training." Emily has a variety of formal and informal mentors who provide guidance on everything from organizing a research project to giving a presentation to dealing with departmental policies and procedures. Her advisers also provide concrete feedback and comments on her drafts of papers (which can undergo at least five drafts before publication) and critique research ideas she is considering pursuing. "Being a professor is a weird job—and it's hard to know what to do!" she says.

In addition to your workplace mentors, it's also important to have your big-gun mentors—in other words, company leaders, industry movers and shakers, successful professionals you admire—who can advise on big-picture topics, such as long-term career goals. Obviously, big-gun mentors may sometimes work where you do, but they are not the same as typical workplace mentors. You want to use greater discretion when it comes to reaching out to these mentors; remember that these folks are uberbusy people! For example, when Soledad consults her mentor, Bob Bazell, the NBC news correspondent, for advice on a specific problem she has maybe fifteen seconds. "You call up and say, 'Hey Bob, I've got this situation, what would you recommend?' He'll ask a couple questions, and then he'll give you his advice, and that's it!" But those few words of advice—like the time she badly fumbled a live shot and he told her, "Don't quit, let them fire you"—can be invaluable. "You get this moment of clarity because you're really confused and really scared."

Soledad recognizes her mentors have incredible insight but limited time, so she comes to the conversation prepared. For instance, she's had a longtime mentor in Dick Parsons, who, as the former chairman of the board of Time Warner, also technically happened to be her boss. "Dick Parsons has been a great mentor to me, you know, but Dick Parsons does not want to hang out with me!" Soledad jokes. "However, I know when we set an appointment for dinner, we get right to it, and I run through my issues. I ask him very pointed questions, and I actually spend a week figuring out, 'What's the question I need to get to Dick?' Sometimes the question is, 'Should I quit, or should I do 'X'?'" However, Soledad says that she would never bother her big-gun mentors, so to speak, with her everyday trials and tribulations, like having an argument with the cafeteria lady—situations that may be important to her but are not what such mentors are good at giving advice on. "I would say out of my five or ten mentors, I would never sit down and vent to Dick Parsons. He'd think I was nuts—and he's my boss!" she says.

GGG Nugget of Wisdom: *Find peer mentors or family and friends for guidance on day-to-day issues. Only call in your big-gun mentors when you've got an important situation!*

Now that you know some basics about how to use mentors, let's talk a bit about how to find them. What should you look for in a mentor? Simply put, you want someone that you respect and admire—someone that you know in your gut can teach you something and share valuable wisdom to help you reach your goals. Again, this *does not* mean your mentor needs to be someone with whom you see yourself being "buddy-buddy."

Once you've identified a potential mentor, establishing him or her as an actual one can be a process. In this instance, the direct route is not always best; it can be a little awkward and off-putting to walk up and ask someone, "Will you be my mentor?" That's about the equivalent of asking someone to be your valentine, said a strategy consultant in a May 2006 *Wall Street Journal* article. While corporate or organized mentoring programs can be helpful and great starting points, many GGGs interviewed had the viewpoint that especially for long-term potential, the relationship should form in an organic way, mainly because the most fruitful mentorships are the ones where you share a personal connection to or affinity with your mentor and his or her career or life path. Mentorships can begin in a variety of ways, from a simple visit to the office hours of a professor you admire to a lunch with a respected colleague to an afternoon shadowing someone whose career inspires you to—as with Food Network chef Cat Cora—an impromptu meeting with an industry icon!

GGG Cat Cora, a Mississippi native who became the first female "iron chef" on the Food Network, often tells the story of how she was famously mentored by the late Julia Child. Cat's culinary dreams started early: by age fifteen she'd already created a business plan for her own restaurant. But after completing her undergraduate degree at the University of Southern Mississippi, she needed some more-pointed advice on how to get started as a chef. How did she end up connecting with Julia? When Cat learned that Julia was going to be in Natchez, Mississippi, for a book signing, she made up her mind to be there—and to ask for Julia's advice on how to make it in the restaurant business. "I just said, 'I've got to talk to you!'" Julia ended up spending forty-five minutes chatting with Cat, holding up the line of autograph seekers as she advised Cat to enroll in the Culinary Institute of America. Of course, Cat began filling out an application the next day. As Cat explained to the crowd at a 2007 forum at her alma mater, "When Julia Child tells you to go somewhere, you go!"

GGG Nugget of Wisdom: *Don't be afraid to aim high when you seek mentors. Consider reaching out to someone you really admire— even if they're very high profile. It's quite possible you'll get some life-changing advice. (Just make sure your query is professional and genuine—not stalkerish!)*

Cat's conversation with Julia Child was an impromptu informational interview, which can be a key tool in the GGG getting-ahead repertoire. Here's a little tutorial: an *informational interview* is basically a question-and-answer session with someone from whom you are only seeking information or advice. You are asking about, for example, how to make it in a particular field, how the interviewee arrived at their current position, what the person's job is like, what it's like to work at a particular company, or even about potential opportunities at the company (in general). Informational interviews can function in many ways, such as a way to practice your interviewing skills, as a basic networking tool, and as a way to gain real insight into and mentoring on what it takes to succeed in a particular career. On the surface, an informational interview is not a job interview per se, because the appointment isn't based on a particular job opening. However, as Beth's story in chapter 3 shows, doing informational interviews—in other words, expanding your network—can of course yield contacts or open doors that may lead to a job offer down the line. Thus, even though the meeting may be an informal chat over coffee, you should always treat it as a business appointment.

———————————————————————————o **GGG Nugget of Wisdom:** *Embrace informational interviewing as a way to gain knowledge, insight, advice, and potential long-term contacts.*

Informational interviews can play a particularly useful mentoring role when you are at a career crossroads—for example, when you've just graduated college or are considering grad school or you're thinking about switching careers or getting back into the workforce after a break. GGG Gracia Walker, the beauty publicist turned personal caterer (see chapter 7), says she

GGG PEARL:
On Résumés

While an informational interview is not a job interview, you never know when it will lead to an opportunity down the road. The interviewer will likely ask to see your résumé, and he or she might bookmark you for a future position. Your résumé should therefore be up-to-date and polished. Here are some key dos and don'ts for your on-paper presentation:

- Do use action verbs; concise descriptions; and, if applicable, numerical data to describe your accomplishments at previous jobs (e.g., "developed a new metric for tracking client revenue that resulted in 20% increased efficiency").
- Do proofread meticulously. Spelling and grammatical errors are a major no-no.
- Do limit your résumé to one page, unless you've been in the workforce for more than five years.

has always tried to have exploratory conversations with professionals in careers that she's had an interest in pursuing. "My parents were always the type that, if I showed an interest in something, they would find me an experience or someone to talk to," Gracia says. For example, when Gracia wanted to be an attorney, her parents coordinated a chat with the attorney-daughter of the crossing guard of the preschool they owned. "We spoke on the phone, and she described her job—she was an attorney for the music industry—and I thought that's just really cool: she blended two worlds together that she loved." Although it didn't inspire her to pursue a law career, the conversation influenced her in another way: "Her experience said to me that if you're willing to put in the work, you can craft your career the way you want—and have the job that fits for you." That's a keen nugget of mentory wisdom if there ever was one!

A few years ago, when she was becoming burnt-out from beauty,

Gracia thought about becoming a landscape architect. So she called a friend-mentor in Atlanta named Lauren, who designs estates, and asked if she could come to work with Lauren for a few days. After working for just two days, Gracia realized a couple of things: First, being a landscape architect involves major physical work! Second, though there were parts of the work she loved, she might like to simply have an amazing garden—but not do it for a living. "This is what people do before they go to law school or spend lots of money on [grad-school-type] things!" Gracia says. "Fear keeps people back from asking for insight—but people love sharing about what they do. Sometimes people are too busy, but oftentimes they will be responsive, and you may have to be persistent."

- · Do use a clear, simple font and format.
- · Don't list your random interests, such as what movies you like to watch. It's just cheesy!
- · Don't use colored paper.
- · Don't list irrelevant experience from a long time ago, like when you were a camp counselor in ninth grade.
- · Don't lie, period.

On that note, how do you get an informational interview? As noted above, if you don't ask, you don't receive! Sometimes, like Gracia, you'll know a friend of a friend or a parent's friend that can set up a meeting. Sometimes, you'll be informational-interviewing inside your corporation (remember Carolyn Hax's story from chapter 3?), and it may be possible to literally knock on someone's door and ask if they have five minutes to chat. Sometimes, you're essentially cold-calling to request a meeting with a particular person you esteem or with someone at an organization you admire. In those instances, you can try calling or reaching out to that person by a hard-copy letter (many people like the old-fashioned approach) or e-mail. Your note/spiel should be professional, sincere, and succinct, but you'll want to include enough details about your background and a bit of personality so that the recipient can see what you're about and may find something in common with you that encourages him or her to invite you in. For example, you might start off with something like this:

Dear Ms. Jones,

I am a recent graduate of _____ College [and if applicable was referred by _____]. I am very interested in pursuing a career in _____. My background is _____. I've admired your work in _____ and, in particular, your work with _____, which inspired me [in _____ way]. Would you be willing to chat with me for ten minutes about [specify her experiences, expertise, career, or knowledge of opportunities, etc.]?

Sincerely,

[Sign your name]

Of course, you'll want to tweak your request depending on context. For example, if you're at a career crossroads and are confused about next steps, you could mention that or, if you've been specifically referred by a mutual acquaintance, throw that in.

While an in-person meeting is ideal, your query should imply a minimal commitment from the individual, such as a quick coffee or a ten-minute phone chat. You don't want the recipient to think he or she has to spend all day with you and, often, if that person does have time for a longer visit to the office or for lunch, they'll suggest it. You will likely want to include your résumé; sometimes it helps break through the clutter if the recipient is impressed by your background and sees how extremely talented you are! Finally, make sure to include your contact info.

If you do score a brief meeting, come prepared. Be sure to research the individual's company and personal career path and think of several thoughtful questions. (See the list of general questions at the right as a starting point.) Dress well and be pleasant and engaging. You want to leave this person with a great impression of you! After the meeting, make sure to follow up with a thank-you note. Some etiquette experts say that an e-mail thank you is okay these days, but Go-Getter Girls still think there's something more special about a handwritten note. Finally—and this is key—if you find you really connected with the person you chatted with, make sure to keep in touch. These may be the seeds of a longer-term mentorship.

A quick sidenote here: if you haven't already cultivated a few mentors, you really need to start now. In fact, you want to start cultivating mentors as early in your career as possible—ideally, when you are in high school, college, or grad school

23 Potential Questions for Informational Interviewing

- What made you choose this particular field?
- How did you arrive at your current position?
- What is the most difficult challenge you faced along the way?
- What do you like most about your job?
- What do you dislike about your job?
- How do you balance your professional life and personal or family life?
- What is your typical day like?
- What are the duties/functions/responsibilities of your job?
- What kinds of problems do you deal with?
- What kinds of decisions do you make?
- How important is it that I go to grad school for this particular career?
- How important are grades/GPA for obtaining a job in this field?
- Who are your mentors or role models?

(continued)

- What qualities have helped you succeed in this field?
- What was your favorite assignment or project you worked on this year?
- If you weren't doing this career, what would you be doing?
- What are the various jobs in this field or organization?
- Why did you decide to work for this company?
- What do you like most about this company?
- How does your company differ from its competitors?
- What types of changes or advancements are occurring in your industry?
- How would you describe the working atmosphere and the people with whom you work?
- What advice would you give for someone just starting out in this field?

or in your first few jobs out of school. Why? Aside from setting the stage for a long-term relationship, as discussed above, you want to start seeking mentors early for two reasons: access and the advantages of "newbie" status. In terms of access, when you're a college or grad school student, you'll likely have access to high-profile professors, lecturers, or industry experts who are more willing to give you their time. For example, GGG Melanie, who we met in chapter 2, spent a frantic final month before she graduated from business school reaching out to dozens of business leaders for informational chats. "I knew I wasn't going to have access to these people in the same way once I left the business school 'bubble,'" she says. When you're still in college or grad school, make sure to take advantage of the relevant lectures, organizations, and social events that put you in front of successful people you admire. In addition, once you've started working, being *new* to an industry means people may be more willing to give you advice and counseling. "There's a 'youthfulness' to your asking for help at that point. People want to invest in you, and they don't want you to make the same mistakes they did along the way," says GGG Denise Hendricks, an associate producer for *The Oprah Winfrey Show,* who has held on to most of her mentors since college (that's about seventeen years now). People understand that you don't yet have a network or experience, and, while this may be a controversial statement, they may be more open to help you at this stage because you pose little or no competition. In other words, as you move up the levels in your career, the perceived-threat factor can make it that much more difficult to find *new* mentors, "whereas if you've been nurturing a relationship since you were, say, nineteen, it's simply different. You and your mentor are friends by then," says Denise.

GGG Nugget of Wisdom: *Just in case you're still not convinced how crucial mentors can be to your career growth, check out these stats from Catalyst, the leading nonprofit research and advisory organization for women in business:*

- *56 percent of female senior executives said having an influential mentor or sponsor was important to their career success.*

- *Over two-thirds (69 percent) of those with mentors were promoted, compared with 49 percent of those with no mentors. In addition, the greater the number of mentors that respondents currently had, the greater the number of promotions they received.*

Now, as a young woman, should you look for male or female mentors? While you may feel you have more in common with a fellow woman's experiences in the workplace, you shouldn't limit yourself to seeking only female mentors. In general, you can benefit from hearing different perspectives and information. Also, some GGGs have felt that the opportunities for mentorships with women in their professions were limited. GGG Terry Taylor,* a media executive, says flat-out she thinks female mentoring has been a "myth." She believes that perhaps because the women in the generation before her fought so many battles they felt threatened once they reached the top. "In my field, I have not found that there's been a tremendous amount of women mentoring other women," she says. "I have worked with fabulous publishers and advertising execs, many of them female, and found that [these women] were always really supportive in a way. They were great colleagues—if not necessarily mentors." She says that she finds it unfortunate that there were no women mentors who were further along in their careers to guide her. "Too many women look at women as competitors and don't lend a hand up. I've heard other women who have felt the same way." GGG Sue Tandy,* a thirty-year-old marketing manager from Chicago, found that her female mentor grew resentful and drifted away the more successful Sue became: "It was sad, and very difficult to deal with," she says.

While many Go-Getter Girls disagreed with Terry's perspective, other GGGs who work in male-dominated professions, such as restaurants, law, banking, or even retail ("There are powerful women in sales and marketing, but men run the fabric houses, factories, and department stores," says designer Julie Chaiken), offered a different reason for her observation: it isn't that women purposely do not lend a hand; rather, as a practical matter, there simply aren't enough women in positions of power around to advise them!

The reality is that in many testosterone-driven fields, the avenues to informal mentoring are still centered on chats after the eighteenth hole on the golf course. However unfair the status quo is, some GGGs deal with it by reaching out to successful women in fields besides their own; others have found ways to work within it by literally learning to play with the boys. For example, Selena Donald,★ age twenty-eight and a Stanford-educated attorney from Detroit, took golf lessons: "All of a sudden, I was being invited to tee time with the senior partners, while none of the other young associates were," she says. "It was really weird, I thought, but if that's what it takes to get face time with the partners, then I guess it's what you need to do."

At the same time, while this may be a controversial topic, a mentorship with, as often happens, an older man can be complicated. There may come a time, for example, when a male colleague or professional acquaintance seems particularly generous in helping you out or in offering counseling or advice. This may be done not in a harassing way, but also not in a completely father-daughter way. Who can forget the *Sex and the City* episode where Carrie's much older *Vogue* editor and presumed mentor strips to his skivvies in the accessories closet? Whether or not a male mentor helps you out because of some conscious or subconscious—okay, let's just say it—*attraction* to you is a complex, interesting subject, to be dealt with perhaps in another book. As a practical matter, just know that you need to *keep it professional* when it comes to navigating your relationship with male mentors. For example, have your discussions during business hours, meeting for 3 P.M. coffee, not 9 P.M. drinks; or, for more informal get-togethers, such as dinner parties, involve your significant other when appropriate. Simply use common sense, and be particularly conscientious if the man is married. You know in your gut when something is weird or blurs a line, so don't let it. And it goes without saying that purposely trying to use your sexuality to entice a male colleague's support is simply not the Go-Getter Girl way. In the long run, going down that blurry, inappropriate path is not good for your career, your reputation, or your self-esteem.

One last note on managing mentorships: once you've found a great mentor (male or female), you need to nurture that relationship. Because most mentors are very busy people, it will probably fall on you to keep in touch and cultivate the relationship over time. For example, you don't want to reach out *only* to ask for advice or *only* during times of need—when, say, you're at a career crossroads or looking for a job. Why not? "Put yourself in the other person's shoes," says GGG Denise, the *Oprah* show producer. "I think if I was a mentor—which I am now—would I just always want mentees to call me up and say, 'Help me do this or do that'? No! That can become so transactional." Instead, get in touch every so often just to share updates. Denise tends to check in with her mentors three or four times a year ("think of it as seasonal"), sometimes to bring them up to date on where she is in her career and sometimes just to see what's going on in their worlds. Another GGG says that for particularly meaningful mentors, she'll send a card if she spots one that reminds her how much she appreciates their advice over the years. "I should have stock in Hallmark!" she jokes.

With all these tips in mind, remember that cultivating mentors is one of the most important components to the Go-Getter Girl gospel. Try to seek out meaningful mentorships with individuals who can help shape and guide your career—as well as inspire you to follow your dreams.

11.

Find Allies and
Advocates

When GGG Phebe Neely arrived as a new associate at Deloitte Touche Tohmatsu, fresh out of college, she wanted to be a star performer—and, apparently, so did everyone else. She remembers going to new-hire training with about forty young people who started at the same time as she did. "I was looking left and right and thinking all of these people are smarter than me! It was very intimidating," she says. Phebe realized that succeeding in this cutthroat corporate environment would take more than just a solid work ethic. A decade and several promotions later, Phebe, now a senior manager at Deloitte Financial Advisory Services LLP, believes that what set her apart was not only doing great work but also doing great work for the *right* people. "I realized early on that there were people who were far more talented and worked harder than me, but they put their heads down," she says. "They may have been a superstar in their specific work, but they had no allies, no supporters. No one noticed how good they were—and they didn't get recognized."

Phebe was aware of a key GGG principle: to get ahead, you need allies and advocates in your workplace. These are people who, when decisions are being made, root for you and report good things about your work and your character. People who, quite simply, are in your corner! What's the difference between a mentor and an ally/advocate? While mentors help guide you along the way, allies help catapult you toward success. Allies/advocates are the people who believe you're deserving of opportunities *and* who have a voice in the decision of whether you get those opportunities. Sometimes mentors and allies overlap; for example, you may have a manager who is both a workplace mentor and an ally/advocate when it comes time to make a case for awarding you a raise. Indeed, while a Go-Getter Girl benefits from a mentor who may or may not work at her organization, she absolutely needs allies closer to home at all levels—peer, senior, and subordinate—to help her navigate the political waters.

To further explain: an internal ally is not a girlfriend with whom you form a clique and gossip and share all the personal details of your life. Internal allies are people who support you and your professional goals and play a logistical role in helping you achieve those goals. They are people who have the power to open or close doors, and you want them on your side. This does not necessarily mean an ally needs to be "high up" in an organization's hierarchy. Christina Norman, the first African-American female president of MTV Networks, learned this bit of professional wisdom early on, just from watching her mom in action. As she explained in *Cosmo Girl* in June 2006, her mom worked as an administrative assistant, and if a caller wasn't nice to her mom, he or she didn't get to talk to her boss, period. So Christina learned from a young age be nice to *everyone* in the food chain. You never know who has the power to give or deny you access to opportunities. Thus, you should make it your business to be cordial to everyone within your organization, from the mail people to the receptionists to the senior managers to the executives. First of all, being civil and polite is simply the decent thing to do. Second of all, karma is a funny thing, so keep in mind that each of these people can potentially help make you—or break you. An intern today can be your boss three years from now.

How do you go about establishing internal allies? First, you need to be observant and become aware of who makes decisions. Then, you need to go out of your way to make a good impression on them. This is not about being "fake" or "sucking up" in an inauthentic way. It's about being nice, respectful, and socially aware and, most important, it's about doing great work. For example, in order to get the most desirable assignments in the project-based, billable-hours world of public accounting (performing audits of public companies' accounting), Phebe first needed to get to know the people who made the scheduling decisions—in other words, the partners for those particular clients and the (lower-level) scheduler who was in charge of making the assignments—and to let them know she was very interested in a particular opportunity. Then, once she got the opportunity, she solidified allies by going above and beyond on the project. "I never said 'no' to any work," says Phebe. "I didn't have any excuses. If someone said they needed me to copy a binder over the weekend, I'd do it. I'd volunteer to travel whenever and however they wanted me to. Almost instantly, I saw that if I did something right and [did] it well, the person I did it for then trusted me and would recommend that I work on a bigger, more visible project." One of her first projects was for a big client for the office, and because of her hard work, the client asked her to stay on longer. "They told the scheduler to put me on the project another month, and then the next year another project came up and they specifically asked for me." In fact, partners and the clients were brokering deals for Phebe's time behind closed doors. "It was, 'When she's done with your work, can she come work with me?'"

GGG Nugget of Wisdom: *Go above and beyond on assignments to earn the trust of decision makers, who will then give you bigger and better opportunities down the road.*

In addition, GGG Elise Chen,★ a management consultant, recalls how she earned a coveted spot as the go-to person for a powerful vice president, Bettina, in her consulting firm. "It was kind of random because she had an emergency assignment and needed something researched by the next day," Elise says. "I guess I did a pretty good job, because after that I just sort of became part of Bettina's team." In the firm's "survival of the fittest" world, where new consultants' success depended on their chances for one-on-one interaction with power players, Elise's ally in Bettina put her on a track to receive the most challenging, desirable assignments.

Sometimes, landing a particular opportunity will require a more strategically orchestrated alignment of advocates, in both internal and external workplaces. For example, several years ago, when another woman at her company was featured on the cover of *Working Mother* magazine, Phebe Neely thought the magazine's focus did not give the full picture of working moms' experiences. While she respected the woman's accomplishments, Phebe felt that the magazine missed an opportunity to represent the "up-and-coming" generation of working mothers in corporate America, such as women who are younger (i.e., having their first child in their twenties as opposed to waiting until their forties) or women who are minorities. Phebe, then a twenty-seven-year-old new mom, who has Filipino and Irish-American roots, thought—in true GGG fashion—*Why am I not in that picture?* She decided then and there to try to be *the* woman on the cover of *Working Mother* the next time a similar feature came around—in particular, the *Working Mother* "Best Companies for Minorities" issue. So she devised a plan—actually, what she calls a "campaign," to garner the support of the right people at both her own company, Deloitte, and at the magazine, to get her face on that cover. "I'm pretty embarrassed because it all sounds extremely calculated, and it was," laughs Phebe.

Step 1 of her campaign was subscribing to *Working Mother* magazine. To begin to make inroads, she would need to know what the magazine was all about (and who was on the masthead). Step 2 was making herself known to the magazine's editorial staff. Phebe began by writing letters to the editor in response to articles she read in each month's issue. In her notes, she explained who she was and would comment on what she did or didn't like about a piece on, say, the guilt working moms face or maternity-leave policies, and give her own opinion on the issue. "Essentially, I became a pain in the a★★!" Phebe jokes. After she'd sent a handful of these e-mails, she got a response from an editor, asking if Phebe would like to join a readers' panel. Then, some time later, she was asked to participate in a focus group that *Working Mother* was conducting at its offices. Phebe knew that this was her opportunity to put a face to her name and e-mails and to come across as poised and intelligent. "This was my chance to make a good impression, so of course I got all dressed up for the occasion," says Phebe, who wore a chic Benetton suit to personify the modern Gen X/Gen Y mom image. (*Look fabulous when fabulousness counts!*) As she gave her comments in the discussion group, Phebe played up her young-professional-mom angle and won over all the editors with her attorney-like polish. She knew she'd impressed them enough to have a few advocates in her corner about being on the cover.

Meanwhile, Deloitte was submitting its application to be one of the magazine's "best companies for minorities." The next step in her plan, then, was getting her own company on board with promoting her to be on the cover of that issue. Phebe networked with her friends in Deloitte's public-relations department and made them aware of her current involvement with *Working Mother*. This was very casual; she already had friends in PR with whom she went to lunch on occasion. She suggested that, since she already knew the folks at *Working Mother*, she should be a part of their submission package as an archetypical example of young, minority moms at Deloitte. "I said to Deloitte: 'I can represent you the best.'" From Phebe's perspective, the goal, of course, was to have allies in both camps of the decision-making process that would promote and support her "candidacy" for cover model. You know how the story ends: Phebe, along with her daughter Maria, graced the July 2008 cover of *Working Mother* magazine. "I strategized a lot about this!" Phebe says.

GGG Nugget of Wisdom: *Think of yourself as a political candidate: you are figuratively (or literally) campaigning for the support of those around you to help you get ahead.*

As mentioned at the outset of the chapter, cultivating internal allies is also about planning for the future: one day an ally might be the deciding voice in whether to give you a promotion, or he or she might leave the company and ask you to come along. Of course, the best internal ally is your immediate boss, so check out the advice in GGG Pearl: On Impressing Your Boss on how to cultivate a good relationship with him or her.

Remember, your immediate boss is not only the person you may deal with most frequently on a day-to-day basis, he or she is also the person who will have to go to bat for you. When GGG Joanne Gray,★ a twenty-seven-year-old project manager from Los Angeles, had a great—but outside-the-box—idea for how to reduce her company's vendor costs, her boss, Mike, had to get approval for her proposal from *his* boss, who was notoriously afraid of change. Over the course of her two-year tenure at the company, Joanne had been proactive about seeking feedback from Mike and had earned his trust by being extremely thorough in her reports. "Because my boss had such confidence in my research abilities, he felt like he could really be my advocate—essentially put his butt on the line—to make my vision happen." Joanne's proposal did gain approval, and she saved the company $40,000. Six months later, she was promoted to *senior* project manager!

○ **GGG Nugget of Wisdom:** *Remember that getting what you want may require your boss to be your advocate. Your doing a stellar job will give him or her motivation (and ammunition) to "go to the mat" for you!*

Now let's flip the script for a second—what if *you're* the boss? GGG Kate Edwards, whom we first met in chapter 3, believes that to gain allies among your staff, you have to create an environment where employees feel empowered. Kate, as the thirty-something CEO of software company Jentro Technologies, is no stranger to being the youngest—and most powerful—woman in the room, whether she's at a conference full of tech-industry titans or at a

GGG PEARL:
On Impressing Your Boss

Feel like you never quite have your boss's ear? Following these tips can help earn you a spot on her A team:

- Pay attention to what your boss wants. If she says she likes short, bullet-pointed memos, don't keep turning in exhaustive reports! Sometimes impressing your boss is as simple as following *her* lead and not veering off path simply because *you* want to do things differently.
- Be proactive and solution oriented. Most bosses have a million things to do. Get on her good side by thinking about ways to approach a project or solve a potential problem *before* you even bring it to her attention.
- Take responsibility for mistakes. If you screw up, just admit it! Your boss will be impressed by your integrity and credibility—especially if you can identify lessons learned from the experience.

meeting with a dozen of her employees. After earning a degree in finance and accounting at the University of Michigan, with minors in math, economics, *and* Spanish, Kate moved up and around the tech world at lightning-fast pace: she began her career as an auditor for Arthur Andersen, then jumped ship to a growing technology company in Chicago, then did a stint at Playboy Enterprises, and next held positions restructuring and developing strategy at up-and-coming technology corporations such as CCC Information Services and CenterPost. When one of her contacts told her about a German navigation-software company that was in need of someone to help build its U.S. business, she leapt at the opportunity, which carried the swanky title of CEO.

For Kate, the same abilities that help her get ahead—such as objectively analyzing problems and using a transparent, straight-shooting approach to discuss them—have a downside when it comes to managing employees. "There are a lot of people that don't like me, because I tell them things they don't want to hear!" Kate says. For example, if a company's financial performance is down, she's not afraid to call everyone into the boardroom and inform them that layoffs will be likely—but only in X, Y, and Z departments. (By the way, harsh as it may seem, Kate says this openness encourages the behavior a manager wants: high

> • Go "above and beyond." What does this really mean? It means be creative, find ways to add value to any project you're given, and volunteer for extra assignments when the team is in a bind. When you're known as someone who can "handle anything," you'll start to receive the best and most interesting assignments.

performers keep up the good work, while low performers may quit on their own.) Before she can hit the staff with doozies like that, Kate lays the groundwork for a candid communication policy when she first comes on board at a small to midsize company. "I sit down with every employee and ask them 'What's your number one concern about the company?' and 'What's your biggest recommendation on how to improve things?'" she says. By spending an hour one-on-one with every employee, she learns critical information and intelligence—"Within a week and a half I can know the six major problems facing the corporation, even if a few people only talk about needing a new coffee machine!"—and also begins to earn goodwill. "As a new person coming in, it helps if employees know that I'll listen to them," Kate says. By giving people a forum to voice their concerns, the employees get a sense that Kate is human and cares about them and the company. Then, if later she has to break the news that, say, the board of directors has decided to sell the company, it's less likely she'll have dissention among the ranks. She may stage a series of seminars about how the merger will impact their jobs or bring in the acquiring company's technology team to demonstrate why being part of the larger organization will benefit them—and the staff will be more open and prepared for change. Says Kate, "I think as a manager, being *liked* is not as important as being *respected*. Employees need me to be able to make hard decisions and to communicate the bad stuff. Even if they don't like me, if they respect my skills and thought process, they'll think, 'What do I need to do to get on board with the program?'"

GGG Nugget of Wisdom: *Establishing allies in the workplace is not just about being "liked" in the middle-school-clique sense. Even if you're not bffs, colleagues will often support you if they trust and respect your ideas, your work ethic, and your judgment.*

Of course, not every boss-employee relationship is quite as supportive as the one Kate shares with her staff members. What if you're faced with an awful boss? Check out the tips below for how to deal:

Take stock. Try to determine the exact nature of your boss's awfulness. Is he or she a disorganized manager? Too demanding? An ineffective leader? An idiot who steals your ideas? Does he or she have bad interpersonal skills? Do you simply have different personalities? Is the problem really *your* falling short in terms of performance? Figuring out what the issue is will help you chart your plan for dealing with it!

Manage up. If the issue has to do with your boss's communication or managerial skills—for example, she tells you to do one thing and then wants something completely different two seconds later—you have to be proactive in getting your boss to define his or her expectations. When he or she gives you an assignment, write it down and then repeat back to your boss exactly what is asked and expected and make sure you have it correct. Ask your boss what a successful result would look like. Make specific suggestions for resources or information he or she can provide that will help you get your job done. Finally, try to compliment your boss for a job well done. How many managers get positive feedback from their employees? It may encourage your boss to be a better leader.

Communicate effectively. If there has been a conflict, the worst thing you can do is let antagonism fester. Take it upon yourself to clear the air—to debrief and make sure you're both "on the same page"—but request a time to talk about the situation when you're both not busy. Don't confront your boss in an angry rant or give him or her the silent treatment. You will not win in a battle with your boss! In addition, generally avoid dealing with conflicts through e-mail. Many times meanings get lost or misconstrued in e-mails, so it's better just to have a face-to-face conversation, or at least a phone call.

Try to find common ground. Let's say you and your boss just clash in terms of personalities: your boss is reserved and aloof, you're outgoing and effusive. Try not to take his or her attitude personally. They may just be busy and stressed out, and so what if you won't be close friends with your boss? Do your job well and use little opportunities—such as asking how his or her daughter's recital was or if he or she has tried that new lunch spot—to try and connect. Or, seek advice on how to deal and insight from a trusted colleague who has worked with your boss.

Go above your boss only as a very last resort. If you see a pattern of bad behavior, start to keep track of your accomplishments and activities, as well as the boss's behavior, for reference. If the situation crosses a line and your boss's behavior becomes verbally abusive, unethical, or discriminatory, report your boss to the appropriate department, typically his or her supervisor, legal, or HR. Know that when you do so, it can open up a huge can of worms, so just be prepared. Don't take this action lightly.

Make a move. If your boss is just awful and you've tried other strategies to no avail, the best choice is often to switch jobs. He or she has probably been this way for years, and they probably won't change, at least not overnight. Start investigating a transfer or a new position pronto. This is one of the reasons why you've been building up all these *internal allies* in your company!

As illustrated by the GGGs in this chapter, getting ahead in any work environment is sometimes as simple as knowing where or whom to go to for the helpful resources, the most coveted assignments—and the "inside scoop" on what's happening (or about to happen) in the office. By creating internal allies, you'll help establish yourself as an A-list team player and stay paces ahead of the competition.

12

Learn the Art of
Negotiation

GG Lisa Cohen,* age twenty-seven, was working at a Fortune 500 company in Chicago, experiencing great success. She was considering going to business school a few years down the road and wanted to gain experience at a more entrepreneurial company to complement her traditional corporate experience. But she was fundamentally happy in her current position, which included great perks like worldwide travel, and was waiting for the right opportunity to come along. "You can always find a different job," she says. "But it's hard to find a *better* job." So when execs from a relatively new Internet shopping portal she had partnered with through her current job asked her to come work for them, Lisa didn't just jump ship. She negotiated for *six months* with the company before agreeing to leave her Fortune 500 job. At the start of the negotiations, the company was offering her a

$55,000 salary. The offer she ultimately accepted? More than double that—plus a unique bonus structure that awarded her more money for every dollar of revenue she brought into the company.

Go-Getter Girls know that when it comes to negotiation, if you don't ask, you won't receive! Far too often, young women sell themselves short by not learning, practicing, and applying negotiation skills. In fact, Carnegie Mellon University economics professor Linda Babcock, Ph.D., and writer Sara Laschever have found that men use negotiation to get what they want between two and *nine times* as often as women do. Consider these startling statistics that they present in their groundbreaking book, *Women Don't Ask* (Bantam Dell 2007):

- In surveys, 2.5 times more women than men said they feel "a great deal of apprehension" about negotiating.

- In a Carnegie Mellon University study of students graduating with master's degrees, men reported starting salaries that were 7.6 percent—almost $4,000—higher than those of the women. In addition, it turned out that only 7 percent of the women had negotiated their salaries, whereas 57 percent of the guys had asked for more money.

- Men initiate negotiations about four times more often than women.

- In one study, 20 percent of adult women Babcock polled said they never negotiate at all.

Indeed, several of my girlfriends and I have been shocked to discover similarly ranked men in our positions at the same company making significantly more money than we do. Why? Well, the men *asked* for more and wouldn't accept any less. That's what a GGG needs to do.

The question of *why* many women don't ask raises a complicated set of issues. In *Women Don't Ask,* Babcock and Laschever trace the reasons to a variety of social and cultural norms, including the socialization of girls from a young age not to ask for what they want and the perception by society of girls who do as "pushy" or "b★tchy"; women's belief that their circumstances are controlled by others, instead of the belief, which men tend to hold, that circumstances can be influenced through one's actions; and the historical legacy of women's being blocked from education and earning money and, therefore, among other things, undervaluing their work and expecting to be paid less. You should definitely put *Women Don't Ask,* as well as Babcock and Laschever's more recent tome, *Ask for It,* on your GGG reading list. For our purposes here, one of the biggest takeaway messages from their first book is that women miss the boat because they don't act out the most important step in any negotiation process: *choosing to negotiate in the first place.*

To illustrate, the authors cite a study by Deepak Malhotra, now a Harvard Business School professor, who once gave an assignment to the students in his negotiation class at the Kellogg School of Management: go negotiate something in the "real world" and write a report about it. Out of the 45 students in the class, 35 negotiated on behalf of themselves, such as apartment rental fees or job salaries, and 10 negotiated something on behalf of their employer (the class was composed of evening students that worked full-time during the day), such as a vendor contract. What were the results? The students who negotiated for themselves saved a median amount of $2,200, and those who negotiated on behalf of their employer saved a median amount of $390,000! But even more interesting was what the students identified as the most important tactic that led to their results: "Choosing to negotiate at all."

In other words, the students discovered that they could negotiate for things that they'd previously assumed could not be negotiated.

As a Go-Getter Girl, you absolutely do not want to "miss your chance," as Babcock and Laschever say, to negotiate by not even getting started. So if you're terrified of negotiation, how do you have a paradigm shift? Well, you may first need to connect with an "I'm worth it!" mind-set, a mind-set where you truly believe you deserve what you want. For starters, picture that you are planning your wedding. You've probably had at least a few ideas about what you want for your "big day" since you were a little girl—and you have probably thought a little about how you would make that vision a reality. Isn't it interesting that when it comes to their weddings, many women seem to have no problem asking, cajoling, persuading, or negotiating to get what they want?

I was sitting in a coffee shop and overheard the newly engaged twenty-something woman behind me breathlessly articulating for about forty-five minutes straight everything she wanted, liked, had to have, desired, loved, absolutely didn't want with a potential reception-location vendor she was interviewing while her two newly anointed bridesmaids nodded in unison. When it came time to talk price, the bride was jumping right in there with a polite "Hmm . . . is that the best you can do?" or "This is my budget, what can we work out?" or "Well, what if I added more flower arrangements?" or "What if I switched the date?" She certainly didn't seem afraid at that moment of asking for what she wanted—in dozens of different ways, for that matter!

Of course, when it comes to weddings, some brides take the "me, me, me" mind-set way too far. The sheer existence of the word *bridezilla*—not to mention the eponymously named show and a host of other wedding-planning programs that bear out the definition—illustrates that when it comes to their "big day" women seem to think that demanding what they want is effective

("It's my way or the highway!"). To avoid confusion, let's make it clear that this is absolutely *not* the GGG negotiation mind-set! What we're talking about is simply embracing a mind-set of *envisioning* and *asking* for what you want in other areas of your life, much like you would do for your wedding day.

Next, for some guidance on tactical how-tos, there are lots of great negotiation books out there, but the one that many experts, business schools, and law schools use as the foundational primer is *Getting to Yes* (Penguin Books 1991) by Roger Fisher, William Ury, and Bruce Patton of the Harvard Negotiation Project. Case in point: when I asked GGG designer Julie Chaiken, who earned her MBA at NYU's Stern School of Business, about how she approaches negotiations, she said, "I'm very polite but very direct—you know, it's everything you learned in *Getting to Yes*." It's a short book, so you should make sure to pick it up.

Here are some of *Getting to Yes*'s basic ideas: you want to get away from bargaining based on "position" in which each side sticks to their position and believes it is a zero-sum game—if the other person wins something, I lose, and vice versa. Instead, focus more on the "interests" of both sides. This more modern view approaches negotiation from the perspective that, if you flesh out the interests of each side, the negotiation can be more cooperative in approach and result in a "win-win" situation for all parties. For example, the authors of *Getting to Yes* use an example of two men arguing about whether to keep a window open or closed:

One wants the window open and the other wants it closed. They bicker back and forth about how much to leave it open: a crack, halfway, three quarters of the way. No solution satisfies them both. Enter the librarian. She asks one why he wants the window open: "To get some fresh air." She asks the other why he wants it closed: "To avoid the draft." After thinking a minute she opens a wide window in the next room, bringing in fresh air without the draft. (p. 40)

The point of the story, of course, is that once the actual interests of both men were revealed—fresh air and avoiding the draft—the negotiator was able to come up with a cooperative solution that satisfied the desires of both sides. The authors argue that their type of interest-based negotiation focuses on attacking the problem as opposed to attacking each other, and thus can be more effective in preserving and even improving the relationship between both parties.

The authors offer a variety of techniques to succeed at the interest-based approach, such as thinking about and asking the other person about his or her interests ("put yourself in their shoes"), sharing your own interests, adding new issues to be resolved, and inventing or brainstorming options for mutual gain. These techniques relate to another important concept of the interest-based approach that many negotiation scholars refer to as expanding the pie. Many people walk into a negotiation believing that there is a "fixed pie" ("either I get what is in dispute, or you do"), where each side is trying to claim the entire value of it. For example, $100,000 out of my pocket for a house is $100,000 in your pocket, and the only issue to be decided is how much money is to be paid for the house. But as Harvard Business School professor (and GGG in her own right) Nava Ashraf explains, there may be many hidden areas of value that are important to one side but not so important to the other side, such as, in the house example, the date of closing or the time of moving in or an extra parking space. When added to the negotiation these areas of value create new ones that, even if nonmonetary, each side can "trade" with the other. In other words, you are expanding the pie and creating new areas of value so that, in the end, both sides can end up with more. Nava says that "50 percent of a larger pie is bigger than 50 percent of a smaller pie."

Another key idea from *Getting to Yes* is determining your "BATNA": your Best Alternative to a Negotiated Agreement. Before you go into any negotiation, you need to be fully aware of your BATNA—that is, the alternatives or offers you have if you don't make this deal. Decide also how you feel about those alternatives. You need to think about what other options you actually have before you can really know when it's better for you to *walk away* (and toward your BATNA) than to accept the deal you're being presented. For example, if you have three equally good job offers in hand, you probably have a good BATNA: if you can't negotiate the terms you want with one potential employer, you may just as happily take a job with a second or third employer. In addition, you need to think about and investigate the other side's BATNA: if you don't accept that side's offer, what other alternatives do *they* have? What will *they* do if I walk away? As Nava explains, thinking about this will help you really figure out the value you're bringing to the table.

When you begin to understand your BATNA, you'll realize that in the real world, you may not have much wiggle room to negotiate in all situations. For example, let's say you have very little experience and are gunning for an entry-level job. In that situation your BATNA may not be so great: it might be another low-paying job or unemployment. You may have to give more in terms of hours or accept less in terms of salary in order to gain experience and build your portfolio, which are benefits that may actually be of equal or greater value than cash (can we say college internships?). In addition, sometimes, certain elements of a job package, such as starting salary, won't budge. As Nava says, "It's called *non*-negotiable! That basically means the company has a million 'best alternatives' to you—and you don't have a good best alternative."

Conversely, if you've gained substantial status in your company or profession, you may have greater ability to negotiate the terms of your employment with your employer. Carolyn Hax, the *Washington Post* columnist whose career is discussed in chapter 3, remembers when she faced a potential career impasse in 2001, when her mom was diagnosed with ALS. Carolyn's column had just gone full-time, but she knew her absolute priority was caring for her mom. When it came to negotiating an arrangement with work, Carolyn remembers that there wasn't really much of a discussion at all. She basically told her bosses that she would need to fly to Connecticut for one week a month to help out with the care. However, when she got up there, she saw how badly her mom was doing and knew she needed to move to Connecticut. She ended up staying for five years. During this time, Carolyn also went through a divorce. "I was basically living out of a laptop—writing my column from my parent's house, or sometimes I would rent a little cottage on the beach or drive around New England to visit a friend and write my column from Boston," she says.

If it came down to it, Carolyn would have been willing to walk away from the job, but her bosses understood why she needed to relocate, even if there were disadvantages to being out of state, such as the fact it prevented her from doing personal appearances. However, as the writer of a successful column, Carolyn had a great BATNA, so to speak, because she could take her product elsewhere. "There was just sort of an unspoken understanding that, 'Yes, you want more out of me, but we also both understand that you're getting a very marketable product out of me. [The column] is good and it's on time, and I'm going to drop off the face of the earth for a few years because I want to and I need to,'" Carolyn recalls about her thought process back then. Now re-married and a mom to three young boys, Carolyn is thankful to have a job that allows her so much freedom to accommodate her family life and says she's lucky because she makes her money "in her head," and not by, say, meeting with clients or on the sales floor. "All that matters is that I produce, and I can produce anytime, anyhow, anyway I want. So yes, my life changed in

GGG PEARL:
On Work-Life Triage

Here's the general GGG perspective on work–life balance: there's really no such thing. GGGs tend to have challenging jobs, full social calendars, and tons of interests, and to manage it all, they tend to think more in terms of *triage*, not balance. In other words, they prioritize what matters at the moment. If you want to be successful at anything, whether it's a job or a relationship, sometimes you have to give all of your effort and attention to it—but at other times, it may require less or none. Think of it this way: if you spend all morning "homing" from work—e.g., making doctor appointments or planning your friend's birthday party—how far will you get on that assignment? Likewise, if you spend an entire dinner date checking your BlackBerry, how fulfilling will that be for you or your companion? By thinking in terms of triage, you evaluate everything you've got going on and prioritize what needs your utmost attention during that chunk of time. GGG Susan Wojcicki, a Google VP and mother of four, has said that she doesn't do any work between 6 and 9 P.M. "No work. No e-mail. No nothing. I'm with my family. People at work adapt," she shared in *Fortune* magazine in September 2008.

But remember: Susan is at the top of her company. You've probably already learned that employees at the lower end of the totem poll often work the longest and most unpredictable hours. To build a successful career, you will have days, weeks, months, or even years when you are going at full speed, and other things—dating, friends, shopping, traveling—will have to take a general backseat. The truth is that these uberintense periods will likely come at the beginning of your career

(continued)

when you're proving yourself or building your credentials. It's just the way it is. Carley Roney, the founder of the number one wedding Web site theknot.com, told me that she almost gets hives just thinking about the *years* of 8-A.M.-to-midnight days when she and her husband were first establishing their business. That's what it often takes to be successful—so it goes without saying that the journey will be a lot better if you at least like your profession and feel passionate about it. Says Carley, "I think at the time the hard work didn't feel like sacrifice. It was incredibly thrilling and such a high to be building something from nothing."

During the intense periods, however, you need to find and *relish* the small quantities of nonwork time and truly make them quality. For example, there may be nights when you really do have to check your BlackBerry during dinner, but you can surely find an hour of uninterrupted conversation and cuddling with your man on Sunday morning. Pencil your forty-five-minute Stairmaster session in your daybook like it's a meeting and enjoy every stress-busting step. Try to think bigger picture and longer term, even if you just think in terms of week to week. It probably doesn't make sense to whine that you have to reschedule your haircut because it's deadline week when you can probably slip out next Wednesday afternoon when things are super slow. Obviously, if you hate your job and it has become so demanding that you can't breathe or you have a longer-term family or personal situation that requires your full attention, trying to triage may not be possible or effective. You may need to find another job or career (see the next chapter, "Know When to Quit!").

absolutely inconceivable ways through all of this. But the thing is, I was able to nurse my mom—and then I had my personal upheaval with [my] divorce simultaneously—but I never missed a deadline." In other words, for Carolyn, where and when she did her work was negotiable, but deadlines were not.

Even if you are the entry-level employee without the equity of someone at Carolyn's level, don't think you have zero power to negotiate. As you know, a Go-Getter Girl believes in her talents and value to an organization and embraces her worth. She knows that an organization is lucky to have *her*, not the other way around. There are many aspects to the terms of your employment that may be flexible. Instead of focusing on the salary, you could try to "expand the pie." Says Nava, "People fixate on the dollar amount—that number begins to symbolize a company's value of them—and forget other aspects such as career advancement, benefits, mentorship, or start date." She notes that the number is "the easiest thing to focus on" but that doing so could cause you to "miss out on other things." Check out the suggestions in GGG Pearl: On Negotiating Outside the Box for ways to enhance the terms an employer is offering you.

Another quick point on interest-based negotiation: while many scholars believe that a cooperative approach is the ideal way to negotiate, not everyone is aware of or comfortable with this philosophy. In the real world, sometimes you may be faced with a situation where position-based bargaining is the norm, such as the average flea market. These situations may involve good, old-fashioned haggling: one party makes a high offer, the other comes back with a low offer, and eventually the two parties meet in the middle, which is known as the midpoint rule. For example, let's say you're bargaining down the price of a silver necklace in Cancun, Mexico, or bargaining up the selling price of your college Honda. In these situations, maybe you're not as concerned with trying to preserve the relationship over the long haul—so you're more interested in going directly for what you want (20 percent off the price of that great farmer's table!). Still, try to read the other person and remember that if you throw out a ridiculously high or low offer, you risk insulting the other person and turning them off to the deal.

Before you become overwhelmed with all these new negotiation concepts and lingo, remember that, as Babcock argues, just deciding to negotiate at all is the biggest hurdle to overcome and will put you on a path of practicing skills, establishing a comfort level, and developing your own style. To figure out what works best for you, it may take a little trial and error. Different books offer a number of strategic admonitions—such as maintaining eye contact, not making the first offer, or not being the first person to speak after you make your offer—which are very useful but might not apply in all situations. Says Nava, "I think those kinds of things are not as important as general principles because they can vary a lot based on situation and culture." For example, in East Asian countries, it may be considered rude to constantly make eye contact; and making the first offer can be a fine technique if you think about it as providing an anchor and influencing the negotiation. Nava believes that more important than specific tactics are the "informationary symmetries"—that is, how much information each side has and the quality of that information. For example, imagine that someone is selling a house that the buyer thinks is worth $1 million but the seller knows is worth $4 million. You need to investigate and probe to get all the information you can before making or accepting an offer. In addition, Nava believes in the "tried and true" principle of trying to establish a relationship and building trust with the other side through simple gestures like small talk and smiling.

- new equipment, such as a laptop or BlackBerry
- gym membership
- stock options
- deferred compensation or deferred pay increase
- childcare contribution
- mortgage subsidy
- matching 401K contribution
- upgraded medical benefits

○ GGG Nugget of Wisdom: *Even if you don't think you're negotiating the exact right way, you'll certainly be proud of yourself for securing a better deal—however slight. Plus, sometimes just working up the courage to try is a valuable confidence booster in itself!*

GGG Guide:
Asking for a Raise

You've been working to the max and it's time for some appreciation, of the monetary variety. Much as we'd like to think your boss would go out of his or her way to give you a reward, chances are you may just have to whip up the courage to ask for it! Here are some tips to help you plan your case:

Add up your accomplishments. Your boss isn't going to give you a raise just because you "want" one or "need" one. She'll decide to give you a raise because you *deserve* one. Thus, you need to show how much value you're bringing to the company—ideally in terms of dollars. Prepare a short summary in which you calculate all the money you've brought in and/or saved the company. Even if your job can't as easily be translated to dollar figures, try to monetize your accomplishments in some way. For example, if you've taken over all the projects of a recently departed colleague, in addition to your own, say that you're doing two jobs for the price of one and saving the company $50,000 in salary. Then, ask for part of those savings: 20 percent translates to $10,000 more for you!

Research your "worth." Before you can adequately assess what you should be earning, you need to know the going market rate for someone of your position, education, skills, and talents. You can discreetly ask around to coworkers (although some people and employers are squirrelly about this) or friends who work in similar jobs at other companies. In addition, check out salary info sites that compile ranges for different professions or even specific companies, such as www.glassdoor.com, www.salary.com, www.jobstar.org, www.salaryexpert.com, or http://salary.monster.com. You also may want to check out the financial health of your company. If your company's stock is dropping or your company just lost a major client or is about to go through a restructuring, maybe now isn't the best time to ask for a raise. (Although, at the same time, there will always be economic circumstances, and if you've really earned it, just go for it!)

Evaluate your BATNA. As with any other potential negotiation, you need to think about what you will do if your boss says no or gives you a lower-than-requested amount before you actually ask. Do you already have another job offer with a higher salary in hand? Will you quit—or feel so rejected and demoralized that you'll want to? Is there any reasoning your boss can give for his denial that will satisfy you? Will you wait it out and ask for a raise again later? There's no exact "right" answer for how to deal if your boss denies your request; it depends on your circumstances. But you need to evaluate your options and prepare yourself beforehand.

Make an appointment. In setting up a time to chat, think in both the micro and macro sense. In the micro sense, you want to pick a day and time that both you and your boss are not busy or frazzled. For what it's worth, some experts have said that Mondays and Tuesdays are no-nos; those days are

(continued)

reserved for firings and layoffs, respectively. Wednesdays are for departmental meetings, and Thursdays and Fridays are for job offers and good reviews (bingo!). In the macro sense, you want to ask at a point in time when your boss hasn't already made her budgets for the following quarter or year. If she's already planned to hire a new assistant and give Suzy a raise, it may be less likely she has extra money for you.

Present your case. Practice your minispeech aloud to yourself or a friend. Then gather all your information and your points, put on a great outfit, and go in there and give your most persuasive presentation about why you deserve a raise!

In fact, Nava knows from her own experiences that it's hard to pin down exactly what techniques make one a good negotiator, and sometimes you can't overthink it. Among her friends, Nava, an economic-development expert in her midthirties, who is originally from Iran, has a reputation of being a shrewd negotiator; she's always the one to maneuver any situation. But when she first starting teaching a first-year negotiation course at Harvard Business School, suddenly she couldn't figure out how to best break down her negotiation modus operandi. "Negotiating was something that came second nature to me!" Nava says, adding that she started second-guessing herself and her instincts when it came to what went into a successful negotiation. After a couple of years of teaching, she figured out her secret. "I can tell you, in my case, I have a sense for what the other person will find attractive. I can figure out what they're wanting and can articulate to them how what we're doing will help them."

GGG Nugget of Wisdom: *One of the keys to being a good negotiator is getting inside the other person's head. Try to put yourself in that person's shoes and be able to express what the* other party *wants in terms he or she can* understand.

GGGs who are persuasive negotiators like Nava develop their own style and pay attention to context. To give you some ideas, here are some more GGG tips and strategies:

Embrace your feminine side. Donatella Arpaia, the corporate attorney turned restaurateur and culinary entrepreneur, believes it all goes back to the simple idea that you catch more flies with honey than vinegar. Donatella says that she has used her feminine charm—that is, being sweet, warm, and friendly—and a bit of feigned naïveté to get what she wants in a negotiation, like the time she was just twenty-four years old and practicing law by day but secretly negotiating the lease for what would become her first restaurant in her free time. "I would never tell landlords I was an attorney, but, from my law background, I knew what provisions to look for in the contract to protect myself," she says. "I was dealing with men, who were mostly older, and I kind of think they didn't expect me to be savvy and negotiate." Donatella would do all her research behind the scenes, but in discussions she played the underdog, acting almost daughterly and playing up the "innocence" angle, even though she knew exactly what was going on. "I do like to kill them with kindness! I see my femininity as a powerful tool, if used correctly." That said, Donatella is quick to distinguish that being feminine is *not* the same as trading on sex appeal. "I actually can't stand it when women try to use their sexuality to negotiate." Doing so is not only unwise, she says, but totally ineffective at the level she's playing at, a world in which sophisticated people are negotiating ten-to-fifteen-year leases for at least fifteen thousand per month in rents. "If I come in with a low-cut dress, what's that gonna get me? Nothing good."

Know their lingo. Designer Julie Chaiken says that knowing the business and accounting vocabulary gave her "street cred" when she was negotiating deals for her fledgling clothing line, fresh out of business school. "I would be in conversation with a banker and he would use terms like 'charge backs' or start talking about the math, and I would get it," she says. "These guys were so used to dealing with creative people who usually don't speak that accounting language, so it gave me a leg up." You don't always need a formal education to learn the right buzzwords. Just doing a little Google research on the other party before you go into a negotiation or asking them one or two questions about their business when you get there will give you some insight into their business, language, and culture. It's about having the information to "get inside their head," as discussed earlier.

Just ask. You know the saying, when in doubt, just blurt it out? Embrace this mentality when you make the decision to negotiate. Julie Chaiken says that she's learned over the years that she can push a little harder—or hold out a little longer—for what she wants. "Of course the first answer someone is going to give you is always 'no,'" she says. "Sometimes, if you're polite and hold your ground, you can work your way to 'yes,' and sometimes you can't. Either way, it's not personal, even though it may feel that way." In addition, remember that some-times it may be more appropriate for a third party, such as your law-yer, business partner, or agent, to do your asking for you. Just make sure you know enough about negotiation to know *how to spot* a savvy negotiator!

Pretend you are an agent. Try approaching a negotiation as if you are advocating for *someone else*, such as an employer, friend, child, family member, or colleague. In *Women Don't Ask,* the authors discuss a study Babcock co-conducted that found that when women were negotiating on behalf of a third party, they negotiated 14 percent more than when they were advocating for themselves. Babcock and Laschever also found that the women they interviewed for their book reported that they felt much more comfortable asking for things on behalf of other people.

GGG ASSIGNMENT:

Go negotiate something in the "real world." It can be anything from deciding on where to go to dinner with your significant other to refinancing your mortgage. Then, debrief below about your experience. Write down three things that went well about the negotiation and three things that did not. Then think of three ways you might improve on the negotiation experience next time.

What went well:

1. _____

2. _____

3. _____

What didn't go so well:

1. _____

2. _____

3. _____

Techniques to try next time:

1. _____

2. _____

3. _____

In addition, Go-Getter Girls have found that with many professional and some personal situations, you'll be treated the best *before* you actually get in the door. That means you want to negotiate as much as possible for as much as possible before you accept an offer. By fully analyzing your BATNA, you'll have a better idea of your walkaway point—and the bottom line of the lowest possible compensation package (or least favorable terms of employment) you'll accept before passing on a job opportunity. For example, GGG Karena Grant,★ a twenty-eight-year-old from San Diego, was at a time of transition in her career, which up to that point had focused on education and the nonprofit and political spheres. She had worked in speech writing at the White House, followed by a tenure as a teacher and development specialist for educational foundations, and had recently returned to politics as the communications director for her local state senator. At the same time, she was teaching yoga classes, competing in fitness competitions, and beginning to strategize about how she would combine her passions for education and fitness and start her own personal-training business.

When she was offered a new job by a highly reputable education nonprofit for a development job, Karena was completely cognizant of her professional priorities and, hence, her walkaway point. "I was very up-front about what I was looking for in my next job. I was a midcareer professional with tons of experience, and I knew what I was good at. But now I wanted a flexible schedule and the ability to work at home, not only because that's how I work best for long writing assignments but also because I wanted to pursue my other passions," she says. Given her unique skills and knowledge, "I figured that I had nothing to lose."

GGG Nugget of Wisdom: *Wait until you have a job offer in hand before you begin negotiating better terms of employment.*

Karena had looked at many of her friends who had great employment situations, and when she asked them how they ended up with such great working conditions, their responses were, well, that they had asked for them! Karena made up her mind to do the same. In addition to a flexible schedule, Karena had a few other requests: she wanted to do a visit with everyone on the staff, including her direct report because she knew from experience how important it was to get a comprehensive view of the workplace dynamics, and she negotiated to have her salary increase based on the amount of money she brought in to the foundation. In the end, Karena got everything she wanted by negotiating on the front end. She worked from home one or two days a week, which actually worked out better for her employer because they had limited office space. Plus, Karena's schedule was freed up to take on two personal-training clients that provided her an extra $600 a month in income. Karena remained quite happy in her job while she plotted her transition to a new career. She is now a full-time personal trainer and fitness instructor.

Aren't you inspired now to use negotiation to get what you want? To summarize, remember these basic strategies before you go into your next negotiation:

1. Recognize the position you're in by thinking about your BATNA and theirs.

2. Work up the courage to ask for what you want and really listen to what the other side wants.

3. If you discover certain things are off-limits—for example, the other party says salary or the rent amount is "nonnegotiable"—try to brainstorm creative ways for added value.

When it comes to negotiating, just knowing that you have options—and a very high worth, thank you very much—is half the battle. Now, go out there, and don't sell your Go-Getter Girl self short!

13.

Know When to Quit

*G*GG Esther Pan, whom we met in chapter 9, had at age twenty-three what many young women would consider an enviable job working as a reporter with Radio Free Europe in Prague. She'd applied for a job at the news outlet repeatedly over a period of a year and a half before she finally won a coveted position that involved just the kind of substantive international reporting she'd always wanted to do. Esther's new job also provided a firsthand view of the surreal, glamorous life of an expat reporter. Still, after nine months, Esther had to admit to herself that she just wasn't happy. Sure, she had a great apartment in Prague and was earning $100 a week in an economy in which beer cost 30 cents a pint. "But I was so sad and lonely," she says. "I was so far from my friends and family, my grandmother passed away while I was there and I realized that I just couldn't be happy being so far away from them at that time." The experience taught Esther that a job wasn't enough, and she soon decided to leave Prague and move back to the States, where she found a job that was equally fulfilling, resumed spending lots of time with her family and friends, and was much more content in general. Interestingly, these days Esther is once again an ex-pat: she is a diplomat representing the U.S. overseas in China, where she lives with her husband and new baby.

One of the greatest skills to learn in your GGG career is knowing when to say when. While there's something to be said for persistence and not throwing in the towel just because something is difficult, there are professional situations and warning signs that indicate it's time to polish your résumé and move on. The key is being able to distinguish a good reason for quitting versus a bad reason for quitting. Let's start with some good reasons for quitting:

You have a truly evil boss. If you're thinking about leaving because of your manager, you're not alone: a Gallup poll found that the number one reason people leave their jobs is a bad relationship with their boss or supervisor. While no boss is perfect, if your boss is abusive or unethical, or he or she is just a jerk and you've tried numerous strategies to make the most of the situation, it is likely time to start looking for a new job.

You're not challenged. There's a fine line between mastering your job and becoming too "comfortable" or complacent. In any job, there should be a certain amount of work that pushes you to new levels, say, at least 20 percent. As GGG Celia,★ age thirty-one, from Orlando, Florida, likes to say, "Your job should make you sweat a little bit, in a good way. Otherwise, you're not being challenged enough." So if you're bored to tears, move on instead of sulking or becoming bitter.

You're chronically undercompensated. Let's say you're being challenged plenty, but you wouldn't know it from your paycheck or title. There's such a thing as paying your dues, but if years have gone by, you may be caught in a dead-end situation. If you know you've earned a raise or promotion, have asked for it but have been denied repeatedly, it's likely time to head to where your talents and services are better valued. It's not necessarily personal. Your company may value you, but perhaps there is little room for growth because the company is too small or doesn't have the infrastructure to best use you. As one GGG marketing exec says, "Sometimes you have to go to grow!"

You have a better opportunity—and don't need your job's paycheck. The latter half of this tip is key. One of the best reasons to quit is to take on a grand new challenge—such as a career change, starting your own business, or even living abroad. New opportunities can be exciting and rewarding, and, one hopes, will bring a bigger payday. However, sometimes they involve a pay *cut*, and unless you're independently wealthy, you probably still need income to pay your bills! As adventurous and risk-taking as GGGs are when it comes to seeking new opportunities, they still handle their responsibilities. For example, GGG Emily Giffin, the bestselling novelist, wanted desperately to quit her job as an attorney, but she made a plan to pay off her student loans and save up money before taking the leap to move to London and write full time for a year.

Your company is approaching financial meltdown. You've been a loyal employee, but there does come a time when you absolutely have to put your needs and job security first. If you're hearing reports of bankruptcy or witnessing mass layoffs, it may be time to check out what other options are available.

You've experienced a major life change. As many GGGs have discovered, getting married and/or having kids just changes things. Case in point: when asked why she left Dress for Success, founder Nancy Lublin's first response was, "I met my husband and was like, wow, I can have a personal life!" Nancy says that in her twenties, she was married to her job and had a major dating dry spell without so much as a kiss for two years. As you move through different stages of life, you may need to move to a new city for your husband's work or find something with more flexible hours to make time for family. It's about prioritizing and renegotiating your life choices, but that doesn't mean you're jumping out of the game. In fact, don't even think of this as "quitting." Think of it as finishing one chapter and starting a new one!

You've gotten embroiled in a romantic situation gone very wrong. You're generally conscientious and know to be extra careful when dating others at work, but sometimes mistakes happen, and you found yourself in a big workplace-relationship fiasco. If seeing this person every day causes you such distraction that you can't complete your work—or the situation is so contentious that you're worried about your reputation—it may be time to start looking for a new workplace where you'll have a clean slate. Just resolve not to repeat the same mistake in your next workplace.

You're truly miserable—or borderline depressed. Sometimes, as we saw from Esther's story at the beginning of the chapter, a job that looked very glamorous from the outside isn't so great in terms of day-to-day lifestyle. Sometimes being successful is not just about sucking it up and dealing with it. The reality is that certain professions may involve a schedule (e.g., late-night or overnight work, constant travel) or culture (e.g., heavy partying) that can truly impact your mental or physical health. Of course, if you're experiencing sadness to the point where you dread getting out of bed each day, it may be hard to place all of the blame on a stressful job. Consult a professional counselor or therapist to help you sort things out, and make a plan to find a job, or career, that's a better fit.

Now compare those reasons to a few "bad" reasons for quitting:

You had a bad day. There will always be good days and bad days in any job you take! Don't quit in an uproar over a big blowout with a colleague or boss or a failed assignment. First of all, if it's an isolated incident, the frustration and bad feelings will pass. Second, a very valuable skill to learn is to work through conflict in a professional situation rather than to just run away.

You dislike some of your coworkers (or some of them dislike you). You'll be hard-pressed to find a job where you like every single person you work with, all the time, and vice versa. For that matter, office dynamics can change with the loss or addition of just one person. Do you plan to find a new job every time some bad apples get tossed into the bunch? Probably not. Think back to Soledad's story in chapter 2 about her first on-air reporting job. You have to weigh the importance of the opportunity (and your ability to cope) against your tolerance for the people—and the pressure—of the workplace environment. Can you still get a lot out of your work experience there despite some nasty colleagues? If yes, then stick it out and squeeze every bit of professional value from the job. Of course, if your colleagues are not only unlikable but unethical and that type of behavior is valued, you should be plotting your exit strategy.

You've only been there a couple months. In most jobs, there's not much you can learn or accomplish in just a few months. It's true: things might be difficult at the beginning, before you've had time to build up skills to know what you're doing or the equity to get the good schedules or projects, not to mention time to make friends and allies and learn the good lunch spots! Promise yourself to ride it out for a while, say, at least six months. While extenuating circumstances may force you to leave a particular job after a short tenure, making a pattern of early bailing will surely be noted by prospective employers. One more note: if you're the type who truly does get bored after just a few months on any job, consider trying more project-based or consulting work, which by nature can have a more intense yet short-term cycle.

You want to "find" yourself. You probably won't experience much spiritual, psychological, or professional growth by sitting around doing nothing. Even in the wildly popular travel memoir *Eat, Pray, Love,* author Elizabeth Gilbert embarks on a postdivorce self-discovery journey that involves an action-packed strategic plan: traveling to three countries—Italy, India, and Indonesia—for several months each and undertaking structured activities, such as Italian classes in Italy and an application-only ashram stay in India, all funded by a sizable book advance, naturally. GGGs who've experienced burnout might say that they took time off to "regroup" after a stressful project or job, but they probably won't call it "finding" themselves. This distinction is not just semantics: it's about strategy and being a grown-up. GGGs know that more often than not, professional or personal epiphanies come through action, not wistful pondering, and that if you're thinking about a major change, you can pursue or dabble in new opportunities while fulfilling your personal and day-job commitments. In short, it's better to have some sort of goal or plan before you just quit.

GGG Nugget of Wisdom: *Really think about the reasons you want to quit, consider all your options, and develop a game plan for the next steps before you make the decision to leave a job you merely dislike.*

In fact, you may be on the verge of quitting for one of the reasons discussed above, but by strategically "reinventing" yourself, you might actually discover you don't want or need to leave your current workplace. For example, Phebe Neely, the Deloitte accountant whose story is discussed earlier, learned that she needed to re-create her corporate identity after she had her daughter, Maria. Phebe found not only that some people had forgotten about all the fantastic work she'd done before going on maternity leave but also that she now had the logistical challenge of trying to rearrange her billable hours and international travel schedule to accommodate childcare needs: "For a time, I felt it was unfair. I felt like I was starting from scratch," she says.

Having been at the same company since she graduated from college, Phebe was tempted to leave a few times, even interviewing with another corporation at one point. However, she knew it would be hard to replace the years of equity she'd built at Deloitte. She'd "grown up" with many of her colleagues at Deloitte, had established networks, and had found the company to be a great home for her to build her career. So when she felt offtrack after returning from maternity leave, Phebe didn't just jump ship. She actively decided to "redefine" herself in her company's eyes. She knew she might not stand out anymore in terms of sheer hours worked, but she *could* stand out as an emissary of the corporation's initiatives for work-life balance. Phebe got very involved in the women's and working-mother affinity groups at Deloitte. She sat on women's committees and boards in the greater community and discovered that she was cultivating relationships with other working moms, who also were potential clients. "My new identity was to represent the working mothers. It became my new way to add value to the firm," she says.

Or take the example of GGG Anne Sempowski Ward, now the president and COO of Johnson Publishing Company, who had turned in her resignation on *two* occasions earlier in her career, only to end up switching to new roles at her same company, Procter & Gamble. The first time she submitted her resignation was when Anne made the shift from engineering to marketing. After graduating from Duke with a degree in mechanical engineering, Anne started out as a process engineer for P&G in their Greenville, North Carolina, plant, but after two years, she'd had enough: "I thought, this is great, but I'm literally at the end of the line. This plant is where things get made, packed, and shipped out. I wondered why we were making these products and felt pent-up frustration that I wasn't more involved at the front end," Anne says.

Anne decided that she was going back to business school, to study music marketing, and she gave her notice. Then Anne ran into one of her mentors in the hallway, who suggested to Anne that, before she left, Anne should look into the brand-management department. "She told me it was like marketing, so I went and set up some exploratory conversations with people that, long story short, turned into interviews," Anne recalls. Suddenly, Anne, the engineer with no marketing background, was competing for an assistant brand manager job with all these newly minted MBAs from top schools, and P&G ended up offering her the job. Anne remembers the company offered her the position on a Friday, but she still wasn't sure if she should leave to start business school, where she was already enrolled. Anne flew home to Detroit for the weekend with her offer in hand, to think it over. "I thought, well, I want to get my MBA so I can do music marketing, but I can go and try out this marketing job, $50,000 less in debt, and see how it works out, or I can leave P&G to go to b-school right now." In the end, Anne decided she would take the job because, as she says, she "could always go back to business school." Anne asked the business school to defer her enrollment, and they agreed. "They said, hey, we don't blame you!"

GGG Nugget of Wisdom: *You may have to leave a job to pursue higher education, but sometimes the professional experience you get in the field is worth postponing graduate school.*

Years later, after moving up in brand management at P&G, Anne again got restless. "I was working on this particular brand and hated it, so I resigned," Anne says. When she went to tell the general manager that she was quitting, something unexpected happened: after he got over the shock of Anne's declaration, he asked her, "Well, Anne, if you could be doing anything at all here, what would it be?" Anne hadn't planned on that question. Off the cuff she responded that she'd been looking at their business and where it was underdeveloped, and if she could have any job at all, she would be ethnic brand manager for the feminine-care category and help them grow their business in that market. At the time such a job didn't exist, but the GM thought it over for a second and said he thought he could make that happen. "That day he created a job for me, and there I was: I became the first ever ethnic brand manager in the feminine care category for P&G."

For Anne, both times she quasi-quit, she knew it was time to get out of her current positions because they no longer fit, but she didn't know that staying at the company in another capacity was an option. "I realized the job I was doing at the time wasn't true to who I was, and I'm not successful, in my personal definition of success, when I'm not in a position that really aligns with my passion and purpose. Whenever that happens, I get to a point where I itch for change, but earlier in my career, I didn't know how to do that without quitting!" However, as Anne grew professionally, she realized that sometimes it's possible to envision the job she wants and bring it to fruition where she is. "It's figuring out, how can I stay on this ship but steer it in a different direction?" she observes.

GGG Nugget of Wisdom: *Don't be super quick to quit a good workplace. It may be time to move on from a particular job, but if you start to think creatively, you may not have to quit the whole company!*

Thinking back, Anne admits that both of these resignations were a little impulsive and says that she was fortunate to work for people who really wanted to retain her. "I mean, if I could have written that script for the meeting with my GM, I could have never imagined that just blurting out what my passion was on the spot would lead to a new job opportunity!"

Indeed, having that unexpected result of literally being able to write her job description inspired her. "It gave me the 'wind beneath my wings,' so to speak, to try and make it happen again." Later on, Anne decided she wanted to spearhead P&G marketing programs for women of color, so she went to the head of the North America group and told him she should be in his group to lead this project. She made her pitch, and he shooed her away, saying to come back in six months. "I think I came back in about three months," Anne remembers, "and gave my pitch again. He said, 'Okay, you can have the job.'"

Anne's willingness to quit a not-quite-right job boils down to two things: being in tune with what motivates her as an individual and having the actual courage to act on it. Anne observes that many young people she has mentored struggle with these two points: "They've come to me because they've seen me pursue my passion successfully and practically want me to bottle up [my method] and sell it to them!" But to Anne, determining the how-to demands an internal process. She says, "You've got to get clear on who you are and what you want to do—and get over your fear. You can't always be thinking about what someone else will say about your choices. If I got caught up in what everyone else thought, I would have been paralyzed! Doors never would have opened."

GGG WORKSHEET

As you think about quitting a not-quite-right job, it helps to evaluate all aspects of the situation in black and white. In the two lefthand columns on the following page, write down all the of the pros and cons of your current job situation, and then stare at them for a minute. Next, in the third column, brainstorm all your possible options for improving the situation. For example, you might list getting a raise, rewriting your role, or taking another job offer as a solution. Then, in the far right column, write down all your fears about each of those options, all of the "what ifs" that freak you out about going for that option. For example, maybe you'll be embarrassed if you're rejected for a raise or you're afraid you will lose all your contacts if you leave that specific company. By comparing your fears to the possibilities, your answer about what to do should begin to become clear. Hint: being afraid of rejection or failure is not usually a good reason to hold yourself back.

Pros of Job	Cons of Job	Options for Change	Fears of Each Option

Let's talk a bit more about the role of fear, because it's a big one: it can take a ton of courage to give up something pretty good for the unknown. However, many GGGs who weren't quite emotionally ready to leave a decent job have done so anyway and discovered that they were all the better for it. This is particularly true of GGG entrepreneurs who've made the leap from traditional careers to start their own businesses. For example, Sophie LaMontagne, the co-owner of chic bakery Georgetown Cupcake (see chapter 7), went back and forth in her mind before she finally left her swanky venture-capital job. A molecular biology graduate of Princeton, Sophie had started her career at a health-care consulting firm, followed by a position at a venture-capital firm in Boston. There, she started to get the bug to start her own business. "I had worked with start-ups at my firm, so I had kind of witnessed all these companies go from the inception of an idea to IPO. I thought, 'Why can't we do this?'" she recalls.

Sophie and her sister, Katherine Kallinis, then a special-events planner for Gucci in Toronto, started brainstorming about possible business ideas. From the time they'd played "advertising agency" as little girls, Sophie and Katherine, whose parents are entrepreneurs, had always thought about starting a company together one day. They'd always loved baking and grew up baking cakes with their grandmother; their Greek family was always one to make fresh bread from scratch, instead of buying it from the supermarket. As fashionable women, they also loved stylish things. After some research, they discovered there was a market opportunity in the trendy cupcake business in Washington, D.C., where, unlike New York City, there wasn't yet a Magnolia-like shop in every neighborhood. They started thinking about what kind of packaging they would use and what flavors of cupcakes they would sell, but nothing more concrete. "We had this general idea, and finally we said, 'We're never going to do it unless one of us quits our job and takes it on full-time,'" Sophie says. So Katherine left Gucci to start working on the business plan and moved in with Sophie and her husband in their two-bedroom condo in D.C. "It was tight quarters, but it made it easy for late-night writing of the business plan," Sophie jokes.

Meanwhile, Sophie was still commuting back and forth to Boston every week for her venture-capital job, and she was reluctant to quit. She was one of the very few women on the partner track in a lucrative career where there is very low turnover. "I kept asking myself, 'Am I really ready to give this all up for something that may or may not pan out?'" Sophie says. She'd been at her firm for four years, liked many of the people she worked with, and wasn't unhappy, but she wasn't exactly happy either. "I was addicted to my Black-Berry at all hours of the night," Sophie recalls. "It was bad: you were basically on someone else's clock because the deals had to get done. You may be 'off,' as in, not in the office, but you were never really off. You were never really in control of your own life." Sophie remembers one time when she was on vacation and had to literally pull off the road and rent a hotel room to plug in her laptop to deal with a "crisis that wasn't really a crisis." The senior management was also a bit lacking in interpersonal skills: there was a lot of yelling on a day-to-day basis. "I didn't quit because I just thought that's the way it was, and you had to be tough if you wanted to make it in the field," Sophie says. "I think the more often that happened, the more I realized, well, you don't have to deal with it. You can do something for yourself."

After Katherine left Gucci, Sophie knew their little venture was starting to get serious. But the tipping point that got Sophie over her fears was when Katherine found the right location for their shop. Katherine had been looking around for real estate, and she was walking through the Georgetown neighborhood and found a little row house that was in really bad condition but had great potential. Sophie was coming back from Boston at the time, and Katherine called and said they should look at this place. They went to the open house, and there were eight other people there taking a look. "We thought there's no way we'd get it," Sophie says. They gave their business plan and references, and the agent ended up offering them the place. "I called my husband—he was actually traveling at the time—and I said, 'Steve, we found the place that's perfect for our cupcake shop.' He said, 'Do not sign anything until I get back! Do not! Don't do anything.' And of course we did. I thought he was going to kill me!" Sophie jokes. The sisters started the lease-negotiation process, which actually took from June to September, and they finally signed on the dotted line in mid-September. Then it became real; there was a countdown to opening day. Sophie finally took the plunge and quit her job. "When we found the place and actually signed the lease, then we were financially on the hook for it. I wasn't going to leave my sister out in the cold!"

For Sophie, knowing when to quit came down to a combination of a few things. First, on the emotional front, her frustration with her current career—and fear of wondering "what if I never tried"—grew to a point where they outweighed her fear of stepping out on her own and risking failure. Second, on the logistical front, she put a plan in motion and waited it out until the point of no return, which for her was securing the perfect location that not only created a financial obligation but also reinforced just how right they were to forge ahead. Donatella Arpaia can relate to this last point. She was sitting in court the day she found out that the lease for her first restaurant was approved. "I remember I got that phone call, and I felt such relief that I could go into work and give my notice! I felt like it was fate." Whether you're starting your own business or changing careers or just switching jobs, the key point is that it may always be scary to make that final leap, but it will be less so if you've envisioned a plan for yourself and been proactive about taking the steps to make it a reality.

So how do you start to put a plan in motion? If you're not yet on the brink of leaving—just exploring your options—you'll probably need to look for a new job or project while at your current one. Here are some key dos and don'ts:

- Do put the word out to friends and start scheduling brief informational coffee chats months before you even start actively looking—especially if you are midcareer; it can take a little while to line up good prospects. Or, if you are thinking about starting your own business, start doing the research and developing your business plan.

- Do keep a suit or jacket in the office just in case you need to change for an interview or informational meeting. You could just wear your interview suit to work, but if yours is a job that's more business casual, your employer may see your new wardrobe as a tip-off you're on the job hunt!

- Don't work on your résumé, cover letters, novel, business plan, etc. and so forth at work. Or, at the very least, just be aware that Big Brother could be watching you; use your private e-mail and cell phone for correspondence with prospective employers.

- Do schedule job interviews or informational meetings at the beginning of the day or the end of the day. Doing so is less conspicuous than popping out in the middle of the day and will interfere less with your current job commitments.

5. Don't disappear once you've resigned. Leave your new contact info so that colleagues can reach you if they need help on something you handled in the past.
6. Don't let your former colleagues drop from your life. Update your status on professional sites like LinkedIn and keep in touch. One day, you all could be working together again!

- Don't tell ANYONE at work you're leaving until you've told your boss.

This last admonition is critical, as twenty-six-year-old Carrie Johnson,★ from Dallas, learned the hard way. Unhappy in her current position as a marketing executive, she began telling fellow colleagues every day about her frustrations and her half-hearted plans to resign. Of course, although her colleagues had been "sworn to secrecy," word ended up getting back to her boss. In her next review her boss came straight out and said, "So I hear you're really unhappy. Are you planning to leave?" Carrie turned purple and desperately tried to explain her way out of what was basically disloyalty to her boss and organization. But the damage was already done. When it came time for promotions, the new girl in her department was promoted over her, and when layoffs came several months later, a pink slip landed on Carrie's desk. Now she had no choice but to look for a new job. Lesson learned: keep your lips zipped to colleagues until you have a firm offer in hand and have discussed your formal resignation with your boss!

What if you've found another gig and are really, truly ready to resign? What do you do? Follow the tips set forth in "GGG Pearls: On Exiting Gracefully."

As shown by the GGGs in this chapter, knowing when to leave a job is a key lesson in getting ahead, and as you carve out your path to success, you'll need to leap into uncharted, scary waters from time to time. Treat moving on as an adventure, part of a lively, life-enriching journey—and just remember, try not to burn any bridges along the way!

14.

Embrace All
Your Attributes

Broadway actress and GGG Kelli O'Hara knows that in show business, your looks play a part in, well, whether you get the part. "Coming to town with long blond hair from Oklahoma instantly puts you in the 'ingénue' category," jokes Kelli, who recently starred as Nellie Forbush in *South Pacific*, a performance for which *The New York Times* in May 2008 credited her with "single-handedly rescuing the ingénue"—aka the young-and-winning-but-naïve-and-in-love female role—"from extinction." And Kelli certainly felt flattered by the review. "But looking a decade or so into the future," she says, "I know that you can't play those same parts when you're forty-five." Kelli has bigger, *broader* dreams. That's why she still works on those classical-opera skills she gained in college. "I'm trying to get enough musical-theater work that someone will let me do opera one day," she says. In addition, she recently came out with a countryish music CD. When it comes to literally being cast in a particular stage role or figuratively being cast as just one type of performer, Kelli doesn't want to be put in just one category. "I'll play ingénue if that's what's asked, but I also have a lot more to say."

Kelli's desire to be more than just one thing illustrates a key point: Go-Getter Girls embrace *all* of their attributes. *Attributes* are everything that goes into making you who you are, such as your personality, interests, talents, and strengths. While there's something to be said for focusing on one talent or specialization in order to build your career, you don't need to deny your other attributes or your inherent personality to try to cast yourself in just one professional role or persona.

In theory, the importance of embracing all aspects of ourselves and our passions seems like a no-brainer. But in reality, sometimes our preconceived ideas of what we "should" like or be like get in the way. Too often young women in the corporate world feel they need to downplay their interests, in particular the "girly" or "fluffy" interests, to appear more intellectual or serious. Some of us pretend, for example, that we only read *The New Yorker* and Tolstoy and not the occasional (okay, weekly) celebrity magazine and sugary chick-lit novel. On the flip side, young women who work in more creative fields—media, design, entertainment—may feel that they need to appear more "artsy" by pretending they weren't riveted by the Supreme Court's decision on Article III and Gitmo or the men's final of the French Open. Well, let's set it straight here: GGGs don't feel the need to put themselves in just one box. Everything about you is valuable and will help contribute to your success!

In fact, Go-Getter Girls like the idea of having many and diverse interests and talents. They like the idea of being versatile and multidimensional. Think of actress and GGG Danica McKellar, for example, who rose to stardom as Winnie Cooper in the hit television series *The Wonder Years*. She went on to college at UCLA and majored in, of all things, mathematics. Yes, she is now a mathematician, who has even coauthored her own mathematical theorem (not to mention a few bestselling books on math for teen girls). In addition, Kelli O'Hara, mentioned above, remembers the review for her first New York City show, which concluded that it was a wonderful production but that Kelli shined more in her singing than her acting. "That put a fire under my butt to go enroll in acting school," Kelli says. In other words, Kelli did not want to be known just for her singing; she wanted to be known as a multitalented performer. Nowadays, Kelli has developed so many faculties that one *New York Times* reviewer in January 2008 remarked that she has "so much talent" and "so many tough decisions" that, for Kelli, "choosing the right path will not be easy." But a Go-Getter Girl's response to that statement would be: What's wrong with having options?

GGG Nugget of Wisdom: *You can cultivate many different talents, and they will all contribute to who you are as a person and to your overall success.*

You may be thinking, as an ambitious young woman, don't I have to suppress my "feminine" side to succeed in a man's world? Perhaps sometimes, but it depends on what you mean by being "feminine." If you mean having a "stiff upper lip" and not getting too "emotional," then, yes, you may need to restrain that side of yourself sometimes at work (see chapter 2). If you're talking about dressing stylishly, wearing lipstick, or using your sweet nature to cajole a better deal, then the answer is no (see chapters 6, 8, and 12, respectively). And if what you're talking about is having skills, interests, and ideas that may be associated more with women than men, many GGGs have learned that embracing the diversity of their perspective can be great for business, even in very testosterone-driven fields. For example, Sophie LaMontagne, the cupcake-bakery owner, talks about a time when she was at her venture-capital firm and her sister Katherine was working at a fledgling Canadian workout-wear company called lululemon. There was a partner at Sophie's firm that was looking for retail investments, and Sophie pitched the idea that they should look at Katherine's company as an investment. She told them it was a great small company, her sister works there, and it was doing really well. But when the idea was presented to the partnership of about forty-five men, their response was, "Lulu what?" "They did not get what it was," Sophie laughs. As a woman who was into fitness and fashion, she recognized the potential of this early yoga-related company, but most of the firm's investments to that point were in communications, biotech, and Internet/digital media. "I felt kind of embarrassed for a while, like I didn't want to take ownership that it was my idea," she admits. But Sophie trusted her instincts about both business and style and convinced them to do it. "We invested about twenty million dollars and took it public—and that was one of the biggest IPOs in my firm's history!"

GGG Nugget of Wisdom: *Don't be shy about your interests or feel you have to apologize for your passion or expertise. These could lead to a great career opportunity.*

Let's face it: sometimes, as young women in the business world, it's all too easy to feel self-conscious about putting our ideas out there or taking risks in general. We may feel vulnerable and afraid that someone will judge us. But at some point you have to trust yourself enough to know that if you want to fulfill your dreams, you can't be paralyzed or afraid of what other people will think. GGG Taryn Rose, who trained as an orthopedic surgeon but ultimately founded a designer shoe company, experienced this lesson firsthand, when she broke from family tradition by leaving medicine. Taryn, who fled Vietnam with her family at the age of eight, grew up thinking she would go into either law or medicine; by choosing the latter, she followed in the footsteps of her father, a pathologist. "I [decided on] medicine, probably because it was just the easier route to take. It came naturally to me and it avoided a lot of family issues," she said in an interview with the *Los Angeles Business Journal* in August 2004. "I didn't want to have to deal with that revolution at that time."

However, even with thirty-six-hour shifts during her residency, she couldn't kick her fashion habit. "I was known to leave the hospital, go straight to Neiman Marcus, and speed-shop the last fifteen minutes they were open," she shared in a 2007 *Fast Company* article. Taryn loved wearing heels but couldn't find any that were comfy enough for all-day doctoring. At the same time, she'd begun to see female patients who came in with foot problems and realized that there was a major need for footwear that combined design, high-quality materials, and comfort. Maybe, she thought, she should design such a line.

But could she really abandon life as a doctor? Reaching that decision was not immediate, but ultimately Taryn went with her gut: "I feared regret more than I feared failure." So, after completing her residency, taking the boards, and some serious "soul searching," Taryn left medicine to develop a line of stylish heels and flats that offered great support. Her eponymous brand,

Taryn Rose International, which combined her passions for both health and fashion, later became a multimillion-dollar company.

——————————————o GGG Nugget of Wisdom: *If you have a dream to do something that is off the beaten path, don't always feel the need to explain it or justify it to everyone. Gather up the courage to walk the walk and let the results speak for themselves.*

As Taryn's story illustrates, embracing your attributes—for Taryn, her passions for health and style—does not mean that you can expect that everyone, even those close to you, will always "get" what your dreams are. For example, years after Taryn's line took off—and she'd appeared on the likes of *Oprah* and garnered numerous awards—it was reported that her family still disapproved of her choice to leave medicine and become an entrepreneur.

In addition, "owning" your passions, so to speak, does not necessarily mean that you need to broadcast them to everyone all the time, especially when it comes to your job. There are some professional situations in which it is appropriate to be "on message" and present a carefully edited version of yourself; think about Phebe's *Working Mother* focus group from earlier in the book: you need to know and understand your audience. Obviously, if you're working on publicity for a deal with a fast-food restaurant, it's probably not a good idea to talk about your vegan diet and passion for the raw-food movement. As always, a GGG is self-aware and knows where and when to let her passions shine through.

To "embrace all your attributes" is a big-picture concept. To do so is to be in touch with your core identity and embrace what you like and don't like in this world, to know what your strengths and weakness are—and how to tap into certain aspects of your personality and experiences when the time is right. This applies to both individual situations and to your life and career choices in general. For example, GGG Nadia Bilchick, a life coach, author, and consultant, employs something she calls the "disc" theory. She coaches clients to think of all of their professional and personal experiences as being part of a mental disc. "You can draw upon any aspect of that disc to give you confidence and authority in multiple situations," she once told me. The disc concept is different from, say, a mental list, because you can think of rotating the disc—kind of like spinning the wheel on *Wheel of Fortune*—to access a particular personality trait or past experience that applies to your current situation. Let's say you're about to give a sales presentation. You would "spin" to the area of the disc that captures your feeling of confidence when you won first place in that debate competition in college. On the other hand, if you're feeling shy before heading to a work-related cocktail party, you would tap into the "fun, flirty" aspects of your personality. You might

GGG PEARL:
On Being Unique

When it comes to getting ahead, if there is one thing that is overrated, it's fitting in with the crowd. The Go-Getter Girl motto is, "What's different about me is what makes me special—and successful!"

Here, list five things about yourself that set you apart from the pack:

1. _____

2. _____

3. _____

4. _____

5. _____

even think about a great first date you had last week! Says Nadia, "Tapping into these past experiences on your disc will help you create another great moment in the *present*."

In terms of your overall life choices, as you think about what will make you happy and fulfilled in the long term, remember that you don't have to force yourself onto some preconceived path you believe you should take instead of a career that is more in line with your personality and interests. It may take some trial and error to discover what that field may be, but as we've heard from so many GGGs, in an ideal world, you're actually looking for a career that allows you to combine all your professional and personal passions into one.

Consider the story of Carla Christofferson, the owner of the Los Angeles Sparks basketball team, who grew up a tomboy beauty queen in North Dakota. She was an all-state basketball player, played the flute, competed in teen pageants, and eventually earned the title of Miss North Dakota, which helped provide her scholarship money for college and, later on, Yale Law School. Carla worked her way up to partner at a high-powered law firm but always retained her love of women's basketball and had courtside-seat season tickets to the L.A. Sparks to prove it. Carla was working on a case representing a production company, and she and the company's owner, Kathy Goodman, bonded over their shared passion for basketball. The two ladies began thinking about how they could take over the team. The rest, as they say, is history. "It was a lark," Christofferson said in 2007 to the *Los Angeles Times* of her initial idea of purchasing the team, "but what I started thinking was, 'People do things all the time that they have no business doing.' That's how entrepreneurs make their living. They do things people don't expect them to do. And it was really just a matter of saying, 'Well, why not?'" Carla is now co-owner of the team—and she still has her "day" job as a partner at her law firm.

Also consider GGGs Katherine Weeks and Lee Lesley, thirty-somethings from Charlotte, North Carolina, and Richmond, Virginia, respectively. The founders of the popular Atlanta-based Turq Jewelry, they never thought that their hobby would become their livelihood. Katherine and Lee were toiling away at a corporate design firm, designing logos, Web sites, and brochures, holding their breath each time the pink slips were passed. "We'd survived about five rounds of layoffs before deciding to go off on our own," Weeks says.

When they did finally leave their jobs, however, it was not with the goal of becoming jewelry designers. In fact, they originally planned to design Web sites for small businesses. As a prototype, they set up a Web site featuring some necklaces they'd created in their spare time. The next morning, they'd received orders for eight necklaces. "Then we thought, maybe this jewelry thing is going to be our bread and butter," Lesley says.

Or Sandy Wu,★ a former architect in Missouri, who traded in her drawing board for a cutting board when she opened a trendy bread shop in St. Louis. Tired of being cooped up behind a desk, Sandy, who always loved to bake, followed a friend's suggestion and began researching opening her own shop. She tested recipes at home for a year, then slowly started going commercial through private catering, a booth at a co-op, and, finally, her own brick-and-mortar shop.

But her passion for "design" never disappeared. Coming up with new recipes allows Sandy to use her imagination. "It's all the creativity of architecture minus the paper pushing," she says. And owning her own business allows her to use her presentation talents in new ways: Sandy does all the branding for the shop, including the Web design, packaging, menus, and even T-shirts: "It's those architecture graphics coming back!" she laughs. Not surprisingly, the shop—and her bread flavors—reflect the same aesthetic she had as an architect: simple, subtle, not a lot of "fluff." The shop itself is very open, with lots of light and clean lines, and features a few select additional products like teas and soaps. For Sandy, her two passions—baking and design—are now in perfect harmony—plus, there's instant gratification: "You start in the morning with ingredients, and in a few hours you have a product to show for it," she says.

So how do you go about discovering your dream career? Sometimes, when you start out on a path, it's not quite clear how all the pieces will come together later on. But give it time and keep forging ahead. *Trust the process.* Everything will gel at some point. Take, for instance, Keri Glassman, the *Women's Health* and CBS *Early Show* contributor from chapter 8, who always had an interest in sports and fitness, given her experiences as a swimmer and gymnast while growing up. "I have a friend from middle school who is convinced that one day in science class I said that my body was craving vitamin E, so I needed almonds," she says. But Keri didn't really think nutrition would be her career. She went to college at Tufts and majored in political science; she chose not to fulfill her science credit by taking the nutrition class. "Everyone said it was way too hard a class for just the requirement!" she jokes. However, after college, Keri was always reading about health and nutrition, even when she probably should have been doing real work at her nine-to-five job in advertising sales at *Sports Illustrated*. She decided to quit her job and pursue a masters degree to be a registered dietician, and while she was in school, she did everything she could to gain experience, such as working at a hospital and gym doing nutrition counseling.

When she graduated, she began working for an online health and fitness company, but with her sales and marketing background, she ended up having a business position. "It was my business school experience, so to speak," Keri says. "I worked with the CEO of the company and learned a lot about running a company, from licensing deals to online marketing to being diligent and following up on prospects to even knowing how to run a trade show, which I'd never done before." After some time, she felt like she was getting too far from her passion, nutrition, and had been working "like a maniac" counseling a few nutrition clients on the side. Keri decided to leave the start-up to launch her own practice. Meanwhile, she'd learned all that business savvy, which no doubt gave her the foundation and skills to develop her own nutrition mini-empire. Keri now has a line of snack bars, skincare items, and a book on healthy snacking, and writes about health for several different publications—in addition to managing her thriving practice. "I had that entrepreneurial bug but also wanted to write and do all these other things," she says. As Keri discovered, her business background and diverse work experiences all came together to form her platform for a career as a nutrition expert.

As you can see, by embracing all of their attributes and talents, these Go-Getter Girls ultimately discovered their dream careers. Many times, GGGs left the traditional working world for something more entrepreneurial, but there are also ways to carve out a niche in a more conventional employment situation (or, say, to own a professional basketball team on the side, like Carla Christofferson). You just have to start thinking creatively. Try the exercise below to help you get started.

GGG Guide:
The Three Circles

How can you find a career that is perfect for you? Try this Venn-diagram exercise adapted from one made famous by author and business researcher Jim Collins. Draw three circles, like the Venn diagram on page 231. Label one circle "Passion,"

(continued)

one "Talent," and the last one "Money." Your passions are things you are interested in and excited about. This circle could include everything from media, travel, history, fashion, or skiing to baking, languages, reading, or chemistry. Your talents are areas that you are good at and where you have skills, such as analyzing, researching, public speaking, or accounting. Try to brainstorm areas in which you have much better than average abilities—in other words, where you may even be among the best. The money circle is for the various ways and fields in which you can legitimately earn income. For example, you might list teaching, freelance writing, practicing law, doing private catering, or working for a corporation. Start with one circle and brainstorm everything about you that goes in that category. Then cover that circle and proceed to the next one. You might want to do this exercise with a friend or relative who knows you very well, to help you generate more ideas. When you're finished with all three circles, take a look at the words or concepts that are common to all three. These areas are probably the "sweet spots" of your perfect career path.

GGG Nugget of Wisdom: *Don't necessarily think of your career as one linear path or climb up the corporate ladder. Think of it as the aggregate of numerous experiences, jobs, opportunities, and even separate professions, each of which plays a part in building your professional success.*

As noted earlier, you may reach a point where you want to switch professions altogether. GGGs don't beat themselves up or fret endlessly because they

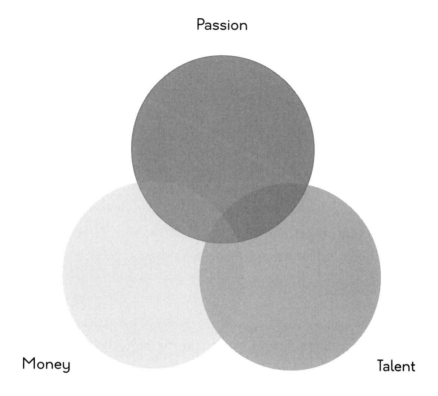

Passion

Money

Talent

believe they've gone down the wrong path. They know that no matter where life takes you, your previous experiences (as we saw with Sandy Wu's story) will somehow play a part in your new path. This certainly happened for bestselling novelist and GGG Emily Giffin, who is in her midthirties and originally from Baltimore, Maryland. Emily started out on the typical goody-two-shoes career path: top-tier college (Wake Forest), followed by top-tier law school (University of Virginia), followed by top-tier law firm (Winston and Strawn). Unfortunately, she hated practicing law from day one. "While I had enjoyed the intellectual pursuit of law school," Emily says, "the practice of law was more tedious than I expected." On her Web site, Emily even jokes that she disliked every second of her law career, except for maybe the firm's cocktail parties. She longed for something more creative, where she could use her imagination. So that first year, she lawyered by day and wrote a novel of the Judy Blume–variety by night. When she tried to sell it to publishers, however, she had no luck. Undeterred, she continued to work, paying off her monster school loans and squirreling away the remaining cash for a secret transcontinental adventure. Soon enough, she quit her job and moved to London with a one-year, self-imposed time limit to churn out a second book. The finished product was *Something Borrowed*, a deliciously inventive tale about a goody-two-shoes lawyer named Rachel who sleeps with her best friend's fiancé in the first chapter, a plotline that Emily swears is absolutely not autobiographical! The book became a *New York Times* bestseller by sheer word of mouth.

Emily always had a passion for creative writing, but for years she downplayed her artistic instincts to pursue the more "traditional" career of law. As she says, law school was her "default" path, and once she got out, she thought she should "do something with the law degree," though in the back of her mind she always wanted to be a writer. When Emily finally made the leap from lawyer to author, she saw that the attributes that made up her personality and perspective could not be so easily "grouped" into one field or the other. Even though Emily chose a writing career over one in law, her attorney background makes an indelible mark on her prose. For example, she's a fiction writer, but she often writes about, well, lawyers and the lawyerly lifestyle. Her experience in the "billable hours" of big-firm-lawyer life also instilled great antiprocrastination skills: she has said that she writes on a set schedule, about four days a week, aiming for structured four-to-six-hour chunks of time and at least one or two sentences on days off, just to stay in the minds of her characters. In addition, having been dubbed a modern-day Jane Austen, it's possible that Emily's critical-thinking background and research skills help distinguish her stories and characters from the array of glib, one-dimensional chick lit out there. In short, Emily's unique background, experiences, and interests all proved to be added value.

As you can see, there are countless successful GGGs who've turned their personal passions into income-generating dream careers—and you can too. By practicing the basic skills of a Go-Getter Girl described in this book, you'll develop a solid foundation of skills and talents that will take you wherever you want to go. Embrace all of your attributes and revel in the smart, sassy, fun, flirty, sweet, edgy, beautiful, and *brave* young woman you are. Accept yourself, believe in yourself, and remember this GGG motto: Dream big, develop a plan, and make it happen. Now is the time to release your inner Go-Getter Girl—and take the world by storm.

SEVEN MORE GGG HINTS

1. Be persistent. One GGG shared a true story about her cousin who was in the running for a mid-six-figure recruiting job and literally had to call *six times* after the interview before she was finally offered the position. The candidate later learned that the CEO's assistant was in fact delivering all of the messages, but the CEO kept shooing the assistant away. After the fifth call, the assistant asked the CEO what to do about the messages; the CEO told the assistant that if the candidate called one more time, he would make a job offer. The whole thing was a test to see if the candidate had the persistence and tenacity of a great recruiter!

2. Develop your own style trademark or motto, whether that's always wearing chunky stone necklaces or having a wardrobe of chic shrunken jackets. GGGs Kristi Wetherington and Kelly Abernathy, the chief executive and general counsel, respectively, of a Dallas-based brokerage firm, said in *The Wall Street Journal* in July 2008 that their style motto is "pick a treat," meaning they select a single belt, bracelet, or other accessory to add flourish to any outfit without adding too much.

3. Don't waste all day dealing with e-mails. One GGG recommends setting aside one chunk of time during the day—she likes the 4 P.M. hour—to respond to nonurgent e-mails. If you find yourself in a business discussion with someone over e-mail that goes back and forth more than three times, pick up the phone or stop by the per-

son's office if possible. The same goes if your e-mail is getting to be more than a couple of short paragraphs. Calling or stopping by is more efficient.

4. Remember that there's a first time for everything—so don't freak out from fear. GGG Alisha Davis, now a freelance anchor on ABC news and writer for *Good Morning America*, remembers being terrified the first time she covered the Golden Globes. "I remember telling myself it wasn't whether or not you do the coverage perfectly. It's about going out there and doing it, and you'll learn something to help you do it next time. Even if it's a total disaster—you did it, and that's the success!" And to this day, Alisha has never watched that footage, by the way.

5. When you dress up, don't be afraid to go bold. I once interviewed Oprah Winfrey at an event and asked her why she chose her striking red gown. She responded, "Because you always wear red when you know you've won!"

6. Start using eye cream, today.

7. Always do your best. When you take on a project, make it the very best you think you can make it. Then do a *little bit* more work, just for good measure.

ACKNOWLEDGMENTS

This book would not have been written without the help and support of so many people. To my talented agent, Rachel Sussman, thank you for your belief in this project and for helping me every step of the way. To my wise and thoughtful editor, Diana Szu, your insight has been invaluable. Thank you so much for all of your hard work. To Sally Richardson, Thomas Dunne, Matthew Shear, Lisa Senz, and everyone at Thomas Dunne Books and St. Martin's Press, thank you for the incredible expertise, creativity, and dedication you have given to this book.

To my mentors, Soledad O'Brien, Rick Kaplan, Rebecca Burns, and Barbara L. Johnson, you have taught me so much in so many ways, and I am forever grateful for—and inspired by—your wisdom, guidance, and generosity.

To my parents, my sisters Tia and Lauren, and friends, thank you for all of your love and support over the years.

To my husband, Kevin, I love you so much and am so happy and thankful to be sharing this journey with you.

And, of course, thank you to all the Go-Getter Girls who shared their stories for this book. You are such amazing, courageous women; thank you for helping to bring out the Go-Getter Girl in me.